NEW ZEALAND
in Pictures

Francesca Di Piazza

Twenty-First Century Books

Contents

Lerner Publishing Group realizes that current information and statistics quickly become out of date. To extend the usefulness of the Visual Geography Series, we developed www.vgsbooks.com, a website offering links to up-to-date information, as well as in-depth material, on a wide variety of subjects. All of the websites listed on www.vgsbooks.com have been carefully selected by researchers at Lerner Publishing Group. However, Lerner Publishing Group is not responsible for the accuracy or suitability of the material on any website other than <www.lernerbooks.com>. It is recommended that students using the Internet be supervised by a parent or teacher. Links on www.vgsbooks.com will be regularly reviewed and updated as needed.

INTRODUCTION — 4

THE LAND — 8

▶ Topography. The North Island. The South Island. Rivers and Lakes. Climate. Flora and Fauna. Environmental Concerns. Natural Resources. Cities.

HISTORY AND GOVERNMENT — 20

▶ The Moa Hunters. Classic Maori Culture. European Exploration. Pakeha Arrive. British Colonization. The Land Wars. Economic Changes. Social Reforms. The 1930s and 1940s. Postwar Developments. Hard Times. Late Twentieth Century. The Twenty-First Century. Government.

THE PEOPLE — 36

▶ Daily Life. Ethnic Mixture. The Maori. Language. Health Care. Education.

Website address: www.lernerbooks.com

Twenty-First Century Books
A division of Lerner Publishing Group
241 First Avenue North
Minneapolis, MN 55401 U.S.A.

web enhanced @ www.vgsbooks.com

CULTURAL LIFE — 44

▶ Maori Religious Culture. Religions and Holidays. Art. Literature. Film and Media. Music. Recreation and Sports. Food.

THE ECONOMY — 56

▶ Agriculture. Forestry and Fishing. Industry, Mining, and Energy. The Service Sector and Tourism. Transportation and Telecommunications. The Future.

FOR MORE INFORMATION

▶ Timeline   66
▶ Fast Facts   68
▶ Currency   68
▶ Flag   69
▶ National Anthem   69
▶ Famous People   70
▶ Sights to See   72
▶ Glossary   73
▶ Selected Bibliography   74
▶ Further Reading and Websites   76
▶ Index   78

Library of Congress Cataloging-in-Publication Data

Di Piazza, Francesca.
        New Zealand in pictures / by Francesca Di Piazza.
            p.   cm. — (Visual geography series)
        Includes bibliographical references and index.
        ISBN-13: 978-0-8225-2550-9 (lib. bdg. : alk. paper)
        ISBN-10: 0-8225-2550-X (lib. bdg. : alk. paper)
        1. New Zealand—Pictorial works—Juvenile literature. I. Title. II. Visual geography series (Minneapolis, Minn.)
        DU406.05 2006
        993—dc22   2005009950

Manufactured in the United States of America
1 2 3 4 5 6 – BP – 11 10 09 08 07 06

INTRODUCTION

New Zealand is a small island nation in the South Pacific Ocean, remote from other lands. Australia, its nearest large neighbor, lies 1,200 miles (1,931 kilometers) away. Two main islands make up New Zealand—the North Island and the South Island—but the nation also includes numerous small islands. The islands are young compared to earth's other landmasses, only about five million years old. Earth movements, including earthquakes, caused the earth's crust to buckle and form New Zealand. Such forces continue to push the tallest mountain ranges upward and are still changing the physical features of the country.

Snowcapped mountains, rushing rivers, glaciers (large masses of ice), glacial lakes, green fields, majestic forests, spectacular fjords (long, narrow inlets of sea cutting into steep cliffs), and miles of sandy beaches make New Zealand a land of great beauty and great contrasts. Animals and plants evolved that are unique to the isolated islands. Most famous are New Zealand's flightless birds, especially the kiwi.

New Zealand is a relatively young country in social terms too. For most of its history, no one lived there at all. The first settlers were seafaring Pacific Islanders (also called Polynesians) who became known as the Maori. They first arrived in New Zealand in canoes about A.D. 800. They called the land Aotearoa, meaning the Land of the Long White Cloud. In 1642 Europeans arrived when the Dutch explorer Abel Tasman and his crew sailed there. However, the Dutch did not stay, and European settlers did not begin to arrive in great numbers until after the British sea captain James Cook voyaged to the islands in 1769.

British settlers began to encroach on the Maori's land in the 1800s. The Europeans also brought diseases that wiped out large numbers of Maori, who had no natural resistance to the foreign diseases. Missionaries (religious teachers who work to spread their religion) converted many Maori to the Christian religion and began to provide Western-style education and health care. In 1840 Great Britain signed the Treaty of Waitangi with some Maori chiefs. The treaty made New

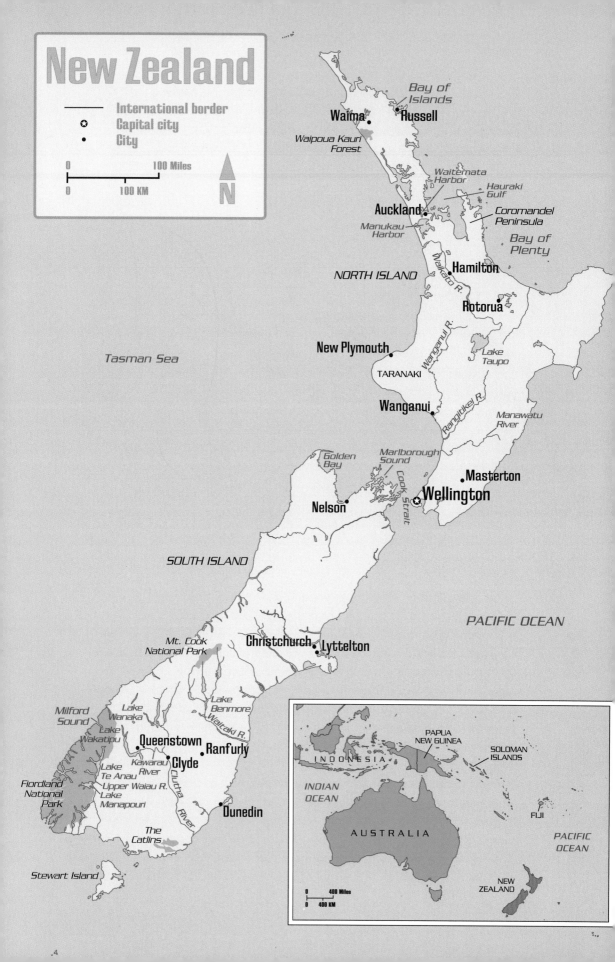

Zealand a colony, ruled by the British government. The treaty allowed the British government to buy Maori lands but promised that the Maori would keep control of their land. The country remained largely self-governing because it was so far away from Great Britain.

Settlers eager for land did not always respect the land rights of the Maori and took or bought land illegally. Some Maori went to war to save their lands from increasing numbers of settlers. By 1872 the settlers had crushed the Maori armed resistance. The Maori and the settlers lived fairly peacefully together after that, but ethnic tensions remained.

The island's ample rainfall and mild climate allowed the settlers to establish a flourishing agricultural society. The isolated nation also developed a culture of self-reliance because settlers had to meet challenges on their own. They relied on each other for mutual support too. A belief in social equality among the settlers led to the rise of a strong democratic tradition. Women won the right to vote in 1893, before women in any other nation won it. Education was highly valued, and in the 1930s, the government introduced social security programs that included health care for all.

Maori and Pakeha (people of European descent) citizens live peacefully together. In the 1970s, Maori began to demand the return of or payment for land that was taken from them in the nineteenth century. There has also been renewed interest in Maoritanga, or the traditions of Maori culture and society. New Zealand society is enlivened by Maoritanga, but land issues and racial tensions continue into the twenty-first century.

New Zealand has been involved in international affairs throughout the 1900s and into the 2000s. Immigrants from Eastern Europe, Asia, and Pacific island nations increased after World War II (1939-1945). New Zealand became fully independent of Great Britain in 1947, and the country began to strengthen its economic and political ties to Australia, Asia, and the United States. New Zealand remains a member of the Commonwealth of Nations, an association of former members of the British Empire.

For much of its income, the small country depends on the sale of agricultural products to other nations. The government works to strengthen its economy by encouraging growth in areas other than farming, including industry and tourism.

New Zealand exports its culture to the rest of the world too. New Zealand authors, including short-story writer Katherine Mansfield (1888–1923) and Witi Ihimaera, Maori author of the novel *The Whale Rider* (made into a film in 2002), are internationally respected. The beautiful voice of opera singer Kiri Te Kanawa represents New Zealand musically throughout the world. In the early 2000s, director Peter Jackson's three *Lord of the Rings* films brought New Zealand's unique landscape to international view and attracted large numbers of tourists to the country.

THE LAND

New Zealand is a South Pacific island nation. Located midway between the equator and the South Pole, New Zealand lies 1,200 miles (1,931 km) southeast of Australia. The Tasman Sea, which is part of the Pacific Ocean, separates the two nations. This region of the globe also includes the countries of Fiji, Guam, Niue, Papua New Guinea, Samoa, and other island nations.

Covering an area of 103,736 square miles (268,676 sq. km), New Zealand is about the size of Colorado. Two main islands—the North Island and the South Island—form most of the country's territory. Stewart Island—off the southern tip of the South Island—and many smaller islands, some hundreds of miles from the main group, are also part of New Zealand.

Three-fourths of New Zealand's 4 million people live on the North Island—an area of 44,244 square miles (114,592 sq. km). Cook Strait separates this landmass from the South Island, which covers 58,965 square miles (152,718 sq. km). Each of the two

islands is narrow and about 500 miles (805 km) long. No part of the country is more than 80 miles (129 km) from the sea. Including the distances added by bays and fjords, New Zealand's coastline measures 4,300 miles (6,920 km).

◐ Topography

Most of New Zealand is mountainous or hilly. A high range—the Southern Alps—extends almost the entire length of the South Island. The alps contain seventeen peaks that rise above 10,000 feet (3,048 meters). The mountains of the North Island are lower but very rugged, and they divide into many ranges. Volcanic forces created that island's tallest peaks. The pressure of molten rock and steam from inside the earth pushed the land upwards, and eruptions deposited volcanic rock. Earthquakes continue to be fairly common in New Zealand, but they are rarely major, mostly causing changes to the face of the land but doing little damage to humans or buildings.

The North Island

The high Volcanic Plateau occupies the center of the North Island. This region contains three active volcanoes—Mount Ruapehu (9,175 feet, or 2,796 meters), Mount Ngauruhoe (7,515 ft., or 2,290 m), and Mount Tongariro (6,458 ft., or 1,968 m). At the northern end of the plateau, hot rocks in the earth's crust heat underground water to produce unusual geographic features. These include geysers (jets of hot water or steam that shoot up from underground), hot springs, boiling mud, and simmering lakes.

Steep hills lie south and east of the Volcanic Plateau. The southernmost ranges—which extend to Cook Strait—form the Wairarapa region, where many earthquakes occur. West of the plateau, mountainous country merges into Taranaki, a dairy-farming area on the lower slopes of Mount Taranaki, a dormant (inactive) volcano.

To the north, low hills and fertile river valleys form the Waikato region, containing New Zealand's most productive farmland. Beyond Waikato are two peninsulas—Northland and Coromandel. Auckland, New Zealand's largest city, sits at the base of Northland, a 220-mile-long (354 km) arm of land with high hills and many harbors. Farther east lies the shorter Coromandel Peninsula, which is mountainous and mostly undeveloped.

The South Island

Dominating the South Island, the Southern Alps extend from the Marlborough Sound of the northern coast to Fiordland in the

The lush green hills of the North Island's **Coromandel Peninsula** slope gently into the sea.

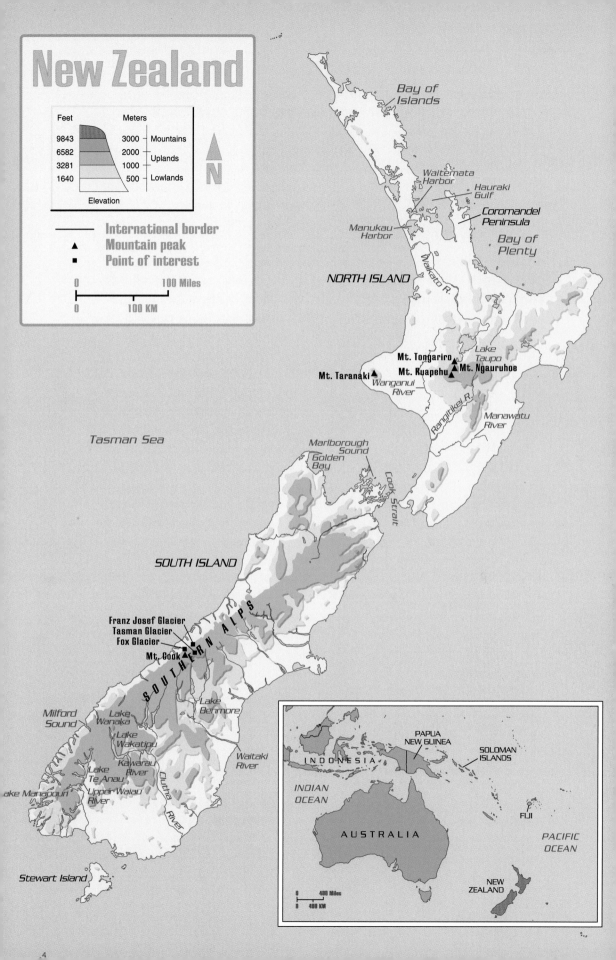

New Zealand

Feet | Meters
9843 | 3000 | Mountains
6582 | 2000 | Uplands
3281 | 1000 | Lowlands
1640 | 500 | Lowlands

Elevation

N

International border
▲ Mountain peak
■ Point of interest

0   100 Miles
0   100 KM

Bay of Islands

Waitematā Harbor

Hauraki Gulf

Coromandel Peninsula

Manukau Harbor

Bay of Plenty

Waikato R.

NORTH ISLAND

Mt. Tongariro ▲

Lake Taupo

Mt. Ruapehu ▲   ▲ Mt. Ngauruhoe

Mt. Taranaki ▲

Wanganui River

Rangitikei R.

Manawatu River

Tasman Sea

Marlborough Sound

Golden Bay

Cook Strait

SOUTH ISLAND

Franz Josef Glacier

Tasman Glacier

Fox Glacier

Mt. Cook

SOUTHERN ALPS

Lake Benmore

Milford Sound

Lake Wanaka

Lake Wakatipu

Kawarau River

Clutha River

Waitaki River

Lake Te Anau

Upper Waiau River

ake Manapouri

Stewart Island

PAPUA NEW GUINEA

SOLOMAN ISLANDS

INDONESIA

INDIAN OCEAN

AUSTRALIA

FIJI

PACIFIC OCEAN

NEW ZEALAND

0   400 Miles
0   400 KM

4

southwestern corner. Mount Cook, New Zealand's highest peak at 12,349 feet (3,764 m), rises from the center of the alps. The Maori call the mountain Aorangi, meaning "the cloud piercer."

Thousands of years ago, glaciers formed in the Southern Alps, and many of these glaciers remain. The 18-mile-long (29 km) Tasman glacier on the eastern side of Mount Cook is one of the world's largest ice masses outside the polar regions. The Fox and the Franz Josef glaciers stretch 8 miles (13 km) and 6 miles (10 km), respectively, down the western slopes of the alps to the edge of a coastal rain forest.

New Zealand's most extensive lowland—the Canterbury Plains—lies east of the Southern Alps. The plains, about 100 miles (161 km) long and 40 miles (64 km) wide, attracted early European settlers because the land was easy to farm. The region is the country's major grain-growing area.

The southeastern portion of the South Island—the Otago plateaus and basins—is the driest and, in summer, the hottest part of New Zealand. Much of Otago consists of craggy hills and deep ravines. In the 1860s, gold discoveries in Otago drew many immigrants to New Zealand. After the gold ran out, sheep raising provided the main income for the region. In recent years, hydroelectric (waterpower) and irrigation (artificial water supply) projects on the Clutha River have broadened Otago's agricultural output.

Rivers and Lakes

Many of New Zealand's rivers are too swift to navigate by boat but are valuable as sources of hydroelectric

HEAT FROM THE EARTH

New Zealand has a lot of geothermal (heat from the earth) activity. Underground heat comes from the center of the earth, where temperatures can reach 12,632°F (7,000°C). Even rock melts at this heat. The molten rock, called magma, sometimes explodes through openings in the earth's surface, called volcanoes. The North Island has several active volcanoes. Heat from underground also creates natural hot springs, some of them boiling hot. Underground smoke escapes from cracks in the earth, and jets of hot water and steam (geysers) erupt from the ground at intervals. In the Rotorua area on the North Island, geothermal power plants capture the earth's heat in pipes. The heat is used to warm homes and generate electricity. Hot mud pools are formed when clay and rock melt under high temperatures. These bubbling pools have names such as Porridge Pot because they make thick plopping sounds.

power. On the North Island, the 264-mile (425-km) Waikato River rises near Mount Ruapehu, enters Lake Taupo, and flows out of the lake in a winding course to the Tasman Sea. The government has built dams on the Waikato, the country's longest river, to harness the power of rushing water in order to produce hydroelectric power. Three major waterways—the Wanganui, the Rangitikei, and Manawatu—run southwest from the Volcanic Plateau to the Tasman Sea.

Many rivers begin in the lakes of the Southern Alps. Two of the waterways—the Clutha and Waitaki—are major sources of hydropower. The Clutha, New Zealand's swiftest and largest river in volume, starts in Lake Wanaka and travels through the Otago region on its 200-mile (322 km) journey to the Pacific Ocean. The broad 130-mile (209 km) Waitaki River forms the boundary between Otago and the Canterbury Plains.

Lake Taupo, New Zealand's largest body of water, covers 234 square miles (606 sq. km) in the center of the North Island's Volcanic Plateau. A volcanic eruption opened the massive crater that forms the lake bed. The volcano's rocks and debris built the plateau that surrounds Lake Taupo.

On the South Island, ancient glaciers carved many deep valleys, presently filled with lakes, in the alps. The largest in area is Lake Te Anau. Its narrow arms reach into the mountains. The Upper Waiau River connects Lake Te Anau to Lake Manapouri—New Zealand's biggest lake by volume of water. Northwest of Lake Te Anau is the country's longest body of water, 52-mile-long (84-km) Lake Wakatipu.

◉ Climate

On New Zealand's coasts, where most people live, the climate is mild year-round. Warm and wet subtropical weather occurs on the northern peninsulas, and freezing subarctic temperatures are recorded in the high elevations of the alps. Some regions, especially on the southern coasts of each island, are very windy.

Since New Zealand is in the Southern Hemisphere (the half of the earth south of the equator), the seasons are the reverse of those in the Northern Hemisphere, including North America. Midwinter comes in July, and midsummer occurs in January. In Auckland, on the North Island, the average daytime temperature in January reaches 79°F (26°C) and the nighttime low is 53°F (12°C). In July corresponding readings are 62°F (17°C) and 38°F (3°C). Greater ranges in daily temperature occur on the South Island. In the city of Christchurch, for example, the average low on a January day is 41°F (5°C) and the average high reaches 86°F (30°C). Average lows and highs in July are 26°F (–3°C) and 61°F (16°C).

Rain falls fairly evenly throughout the year in New Zealand. The average for the whole country is 25 to 60 inches (64 to 152 centimeters) annually. On the South Island, however, the high mountains make a barrier that affects the way rainfall is distributed to various regions. Most air masses move in from the west. Blocked by the alps, the air rises, dropping its moisture on the coast and western slopes. Thus the coastal rain forest at the western base of the alps receives more than 200 inches (508 cm) of rain annually. Because the air loses moisture as it crosses the mountains, some parts of Otago on the eastern side get only 13 inches (33 cm) of precipitation each year. Snow is common only in the high mountains.

Flora and Fauna

Because of the islands' isolation, most of the native plants and animals are endemic to New Zealand—that is, they are not found anywhere else on earth. More than two thousand varieties of ferns, evergreens, and flowering plants are native to New Zealand. Before humans arrived, 80 percent of the islands was densely forested. The Maori burned about one-third of the trees to clear land for farming, to obtain timber, and to force hunted animals into the open. European settlers removed an additional one-third of the forests.

New Zealand's native evergreens include the rimu, kahikatea, totara, and kauri. The soft-wooded totara was used by the Maori to make war canoes. The giant kauri can live for two thousand years, reaching 200 feet (61 m) in height. Great stands of the tree once grew on the northern peninsulas. In the 1800s, however, shipbuilders prized this timber so highly that loggers nearly destroyed the kauri forests. Laws protect remaining stands of the tree. Native beech forests still occupy regions in the western alps on the South Island.

LORD OF THE FOREST

Tane Mahuta means Lord of the Forest in Maori. It is the name of the largest kauri tree in New Zealand. It is 171 feet (52 m) high and 40 feet (12 m) around. It is at least 1,200 years old. Tane Mahuta lives in the Waipoua Kauri Forest, a preserve of the huge trees on the west coast of the North Island. The kauris are not cut down except for special occasions, such as the carving of a Maori canoe.

Broad-leaved trees—such as the karaka and red-blossomed pohutukawa—grow in coastal forests. Many varieties of ferns—some 50 feet (15 m) tall—cover forest floors. These primitive plants evolved millions of years ago, when dinosaurs roamed the earth, and they are found all over New Zealand. The silver tree fern is the country's official emblem. In the mountains, vegetation has adapted to cold, windy conditions. Plant species that thrive in high elevations include daisies, nicotiana (a flowering shrub), and cushion plants. An unusual coastal plant is the cabbage tree—a giant lily with spear-shaped foliage.

The **tuatara reptile** and the kiwi bird *(inset)* are just two of New Zealand's many native species. The tuatara has an undeveloped third eye and may live for close to one hundred years.

Because the islands of New Zealand are far from continents where mammals evolved, there are no large land mammals native to New Zealand. Only one mammal, the bat, is a native. There are three kinds of reptiles—skinks, geckos, and tuatara. The tuatara, a lizardlike reptile, survives from the age of the dinosaurs (about 220 million years ago). Many kinds of insects live in the islands, including more than one hundred wetas, large invertebrates (animals without backbones) that resemble wingless crickets. There are no snakes.

In the absence of predators (animals that hunt and eat other animals), many flightless birds evolved in New Zealand. Perhaps the most remarkable bird to live on the islands was the giant moa. By the seventeenth century, however, the Maori had hunted this 10-foot-tall (3 m) plant eater to extinction. A small relative of the moa—the kiwi—has become a national symbol. In fact, New Zealanders call themselves Kiwis after the shy brown bird of their forests.

Among New Zealand's other flightless birds are the kakapo (the world's only flightless parrot), the weka (wood hen), the pukeko (swamp hen), and the takahe. The takahe is a large bird with blue and green feathers, a red bill, and red legs. Thirteen kinds of penguins live in coastal waters, including the little blue penguin, the smallest species of penguin. Many species of birds that fly died out after humans began cutting New Zealand's forests. Among those that survived are two frequently heard songbirds, the tui and the bellbird. The tui has a melodious song, but it is also a talented mimic, imitating the sounds of other birds—or even cats!

Many marine mammals can be found in New Zealand waters. Thirty-five species of whales and dolphins live there. The Hectors dolphin is found only in New Zealand waters. People once hunted whales and seals for their oil and skins. In modern times, tourists enjoy watching whales, seals, sea lions, and other marine life.

Environmental Concerns

Humans and other nonnative mammals introduced to the islands have caused devastation to New Zealand's unique wildlife. The Maori introduced dogs and rats to the islands, and Europeans brought more species that damaged the sheltered islands. European deer, goats, rabbits, and an estimated 70 million possums eat native plants and destroy the places birds live. Predatory animals such as cats and stoats (ermines, a kind of weasel) have hunted some animals almost to extinction.

The widespread destruction of forests by nineteenth century settlers desiring pastureland caused serious erosion (the wearing away of soil) in some parts of New Zealand. The practice also destroyed the habitats of some animals that existed nowhere else in the world. In the twenty-first century, most of the remaining indigenous forest is protected. The forestry industry relies on tree plantations (large farms) for timber and wood products, rather than cutting down natural forests.

New Zealand's islands are continually ventilated by ocean winds, keeping the air fresh. Nonetheless, air pollution from vehicles, industry, and agriculture is high in some parts of the country. Auckland has high levels of carbon dioxide from vehicle exhaust. New Zealand's air pollution creates greenhouse gases (gas that erodes the ozone layer shielding the planet), which affects the global environment.

Water and thermal (heat from the earth) power plants are safe, self-renewing, and nonpolluting forms of energy production. Hydroelectricity supplies about 70 percent of New Zealand's electricity needs. New Zealand does not allow any form of nuclear power to be used or generated in the country, so this potential danger is not a threat to the environment.

Among present-day New Zealanders, concern about the environment is very high . Conservationists, often working cooperatively with the governmental Department of Conservation (DOC), have achieved considerable success in protecting the country's unusual plants and animals. For instance, conservationists have removed pests such as stoats from certain offshore islands and reintroduced endangered native species, such as the flightless kakapo. The DOC maintains fourteen national parks and hundreds of forest and marine parks and wildlife

Author Douglas Adams once wrote that the **kakapo** "has a look of serenely innocent incomprehension that makes you want to hug it and tell it that everything will be all right, though you know that it probably will not be."

reserves. Public pressure to protect the natural environment continues. Stewart Island was made a national park in 2001.

◉ Natural Resources

Land is the most important resource for this agricultural country. Though the soil is not highly fertile, ample rainfall, a mild year-round climate, and scientific farming methods—including the use of fertilizers and farm machines—allow for lush pasturelands to feed millions of sheep and cattle. About 29 percent of the country's land is forest, much of it preserved. The timber industry relies on careful management of human-made tree plantations.

Plentiful and regular rainfall provides New Zealand with freshwater. New Zealand's swift rivers are also important and reliable sources of hydroelectric power. Large lakes act as reservoirs (storage) for rivers with major power stations. Coastal waters provide New Zealand with an abundance of sea life. Fishing is an important industry, and marine animals are major tourist attractions.

A wide variety of minerals are present but mostly only in small quantities. Sands that contain iron are processed to produce iron and steel. Gold is the most valuable metallic mineral. Non-metallic minerals, including coal, clay, and limestone, are important to industry. Exploration of other minerals is gradually expanding. Natural gas fields supply much of the country's power. There are also offshore petroleum fields.

Cities

With 84 percent of its people living in cities, New Zealand is one of the most urbanized of modern countries. Auckland is the most populated urban area in the country. Ranking next in size are Wellington, Christchurch, Hamilton, and Dunedin.

AUCKLAND, with a population of 1.2 million, is New Zealand's leading financial, commercial, and industrial center. Nearly surrounded by water, the city occupies a narrow neck of land west of the Hauraki Gulf. Waitemata Harbor and Manukau Harbor provide access for ships.

Long before European colonists arrived, Maori groups discovered the fertile soil of the Auckland area. They built fortresses on the sides and in the craters of extinct volcanoes in the region. After Europeans settled there, the availability of flatland and a fine harbor drew industry to the site. In recent decades, job opportunities in Auckland have attracted thousands of Pacific Islanders as well as people from Asia and other parts of New Zealand.

WELLINGTON, New Zealand's capital city, is the southernmost national capital in the world. It lies on the southern tip of the North Island on a deep, circular harbor. Steep hills surround the city. The hills are bounded by active fault lines (fractures in the earth's crust), which have the potential to cause earthquakes. Many of Wellington's 415,700 residents work for the national government, but a variety of businesses also operate in the capital. Parliament (New Zealand's legislature) meets in a modern building known as the Beehive because of its round shape, which is an architectural symbol of the country.

CHRISTCHURCH (population 331,400) is the biggest urban center on the South Island. The Canterbury Association in Britain—an association of religious and political officials—helped found the city in 1850. One of

The Maori call **Auckland** Tamaki Makau Rau, or City of One Hundred Lovers, because throughout New Zealand's history the city has been desired and conquered by many different people. Visit www.vgsbooks.com for links to more information about what there is to see and do in New Zealand's cities.

the group's goals was to build a city with a distinctly British appearance, complete with an Anglican (Church of England) cathedral. Fertile flat farmland and good grazing for sheep made early settlers wealthy. The city is famous for its carefully tended gardens. Lying near the eastern coast almost halfway down the South Island, Christchurch is the industrial center of the Canterbury Plains. With fine port facilities at nearby Lyttelton and an international airport, the city also serves as a base for Antarctic research.

HAMILTON Located 65 miles (105 km) south of Auckland, Hamilton is the largest inland city in New Zealand, with a population of 132,100. On the banks of the Waikato River, Hamilton serves as a hub for the Waikato region's dairy and beef farms. The city contains several agricultural research facilities and many industries. The Hamilton Zoo is one of the country's best zoos.

DUNEDIN (population 110,800) lies 200 miles (322 km) south of Christchurch. Scottish immigrants settled the city in 1848. (Dunedin is the traditional Scottish name for Edinburgh, the capital of Scotland.) In the 1860s, prospectors flocked to Dunedin when gold was discovered in the Otago region. The city flourished as New Zealand's financial hub until gold supplies ran out toward the end of the decade. Its citizens then turned to farming and industry, but much of the grand nineteenth-century architecture survives. Dunedin is the home of the University of Otago, the oldest of New Zealand's six universities.

HISTORY AND GOVERNMENT

The first inhabitants of New Zealand were the Maori. The Maori were expert sailors who migrated from eastern Polynesia sometime between A.D. 700 and 1000. Their ancestral island, Hawaiki, was probably near Tahiti. Historians do not know whether the Maori found New Zealand by accident—by being blown off course while seeking another destination—or by plan, nor have researchers determined whether the Maori came in one large migration or in numerous voyages.

The Maori had no written language, but they did have a rich storytelling tradition. According to legend, a Polynesian fisher named Kupe discovered the islands around 925. He called them Aotearoa, meaning the Land of the Long White Cloud. Kupe explored Aotearoa, but finding the region uninhabited and disliking the cool climate, he returned to Hawaiki. Generations of Maori heard Kupe's stories of Aotearoa. Eventually some of his people set out in large oceangoing canoes to settle the faraway islands.

The Moa Hunters

Although scholars respect the Maori legends, they rely on site excavations (digging to uncover ancient remains), language studies, and comparisons with other Polynesian peoples to learn about the settlement of New Zealand. Archaeologists have determined that to survive, most of the earliest Maori in New Zealand fished and hunted the giant, flightless moa and other birds. These Maori—called Moa Hunters—followed a simple way of life.

Most of the early Maori lived on the South Island, where the largest species of moa were plentiful. By 1100 the Moa Hunter culture was well established. In the northern parts of the North Island, however, Maori groups had begun to develop a society based on agriculture. They grew starchy root crops they had brought from Polynesia—kumaras (sweet potatoes), taros, and yams. They also cultivated native ferns, whose roots are nourishing.

In the 1300s, food supplies in Aotearoa began to dwindle. The number of moa decreased, and Moa Hunters burned wooded areas to dislodge the birds. As forests disappeared, rain washed soil from hills into rivers, ruining fishing areas. In addition, the weather grew cold and stormy when a period called the Little Ice Age arrived during the 1500s. The soil of farmed plots lost their fertility, and storms made it hard to clear additional land. As conditions worsened, the Moa Hunter culture declined.

Classic Maori Culture

In the north, however, the Maori who relied on agriculture were able to meet the challenge of a colder, stormier climate. They learned to use storage pits to preserve food supplies during the winter, and they designed buildings and clothing to protect themselves from the weather. These groups developed a way of life that archaeologists call the Classic Maori culture.

About fifty *iwi* (Maori groups) established themselves in New Zealand. Within each iwi, extended (closely related) families formed *hapu*—or clans—and held land in common. In most hapu, members lived in houses within or close to a *pa*—an area protected by natural boundaries, wooden stockades, and terraces. Families retreated to the pa during warfare.

By the eighteenth century, the Maori on the North Island were skilled farmers, builders, and weavers. Using stone tools, they also excelled at wood carving. The Maori developed a religion that regarded many places, people, events, and features of the land and sea as sacred. Proper respect for ancestors was an important spiritual value. It was believed that the spirits of the dead returned to the spiritual homeland of Hawaiki. Hospitality was another feature of Maori belief, reflecting the view that people are the most important thing in the world. Land was also highly valued. Each Maori group's prestige was linked to land and geographical features such as mountains and rivers, some of which were *tapu* (sacred). Warriors were willing to protect the land with their lives.

As population and land needs increased, war became an established part of Maori society. By fighting, warriors gained prestige and practiced *utu*—revenge for wrongs committed against their people. Raids went back and forth, and so some iwi were in almost constant warfare. Fighting was hand to hand. Weapons included hand spears and clubs, including the *mere*, a short club made of greenstone (a jadelike stone). Victors in battle insulted their enemies by eating those they had slain. It was also believed that victors gained some of the enemies' life force or power by eating them. Captives from defeated hapu became slaves in other hapu.

The **mere** was the simplest of all Maori *patu*, or war weapons. The one at right is made of jade.

European Exploration

The Maori's first contact with non-Polynesian peoples probably occurred in 1642 when the Dutch navigator Abel Tasman reached Golden Bay on the northwestern corner of the South Island. The Maori used canoes to attack one of the expedition's landing boats, and lives were lost on both sides. Tasman sailed away without setting foot on the islands, which the Dutch government later named Nieuw Zeeland, after the Dutch province Zeeland. More than 125 years passed before the Maori again saw Europeans.

In 1769 the British navy sent Captain James Cook in the ship *Endeavour* to explore the South Pacific. Cook arrived in New Zealand in October 1769 and encountered Maori at many of his landing sites. Unlike Tasman's experience with Maori, these meetings were usually friendly. Cook came to admire the people's resourcefulness.

Captain James Cook

A Polynesian who had joined the *Endeavour* in Tahiti was able to interpret the Maori language, enabling the crew to trade goods with the local people. The expedition's scientists collected samples of plant life. Cook spent 176 days charting New Zealand and produced an accurate map of the main islands. The captain and others in his party published accounts of New Zealand after this journey and after two later voyages to the South Pacific.

Pakeha Arrive

For twenty years after Cook's voyages, few Pakeha landed in New Zealand. But in the 1790s, a growing demand in Europe for sealskins and whale oil sent European seal-hunting and whaling ships to New Zealand's coastal waters. Sailors anchored their vessels in the Bay of Islands on the eastern coast of the Northland Peninsula, and sealing and whaling villages sprang up along its harbors in the early 1800s.

The region's kauri trees provided long, sturdy timbers for ship masts, and native flax plants yielded fiber for rope. Traders from New South Wales, Australia—a British colony—began sailing to New Zealand. Soon ships from the United States and European countries were also arriving in the Bay of Islands. Trade created jobs for many Maori. They cut timber, prepared flax, and served on ships' crews.

Although Cook had explored New Zealand for Britain, that nation showed little interest at first in colonizing (ruling) the area. With no authorities to make or enforce regulations, Kororareka (the first British capital and present-day Russell) and other coastal villages on the Bay of Islands earned a reputation for lawlessness. Australia served as a prison colony for criminals from the British Isles, and among the inhabitants of these outposts were escaped convicts from Australia and runaway sailors.

A different type of Pakeha soon arrived in New Zealand, however. Samuel Marsden, a Church of England missionary in Australia, established the first Christian mission (religious community with church and school) in the Bay of Islands area in 1814. He recruited a staff from Britain to teach the Maori and to convert them to Christianity. When Henry Williams arrived to direct the mission in 1823, he translated the Bible into Maori and taught reading and writing. The Maori were eager to learn to read and write, finding it a novel and interesting pastime. Using the Bible to learn to read, the Maori also absorbed Christian teachings, and by 1830 a few Maori had converted to Christianity. Though most Maori did not wholly reject traditional ways, new technology, literacy, and beliefs began to gradually change the Maori way of life. The missionaries also worked to stop Maori traditions of warfare, cannibalism (eating human flesh), and slavery, and they were sometimes welcomed by the Maori as peacemakers between iwi.

The other Pakeha with whom the Maori dealt—traders, sailors, and adventurers—affected Maori society more quickly. Those Europeans introduced guns, new diseases, and liquor into New Zealand. Guns made some Maori leaders—including Hongi Hika, a chief in the Bay of Islands—very powerful. With a force of two thousand warriors, Hongi Hika attacked other North Island Maori to settle disputes.

Infectious diseases, including measles and tuberculosis, posed another threat to the Maori, who had lived for centuries in isolation and had no natural protection against illnesses brought by Europeans. As guns, sickness, and alcohol spread among the Maori, their population—which probably numbered about 250,000 when Cook came to New Zealand—declined rapidly.

British Colonization

Fewer than two thousand Europeans lived in New Zealand in the late 1830s, but speculators (people who buy land to make a profit later) scrambled to obtain Maori land. Representatives of the New Zealand Company, founded in Britain by Edward Gibbon Wakefield, were among the eager buyers who wanted to exploit New Zealand's natural resources. Wakefield, who wanted to promote the orderly settlement of New Zealand, raised money by selling shares in the company to wealthy investors. With those funds, the company purchased land and arranged for the transportation of British tradespeople and laborers. They would be the workers in the company's settlements. Most British settlers were working- or middle-class immigrants from England and Scotland, but a small number came from Ireland.

As settlers, missionaries, and businesspeople sought to create an ordered society, they wanted New Zealand to become a colony under British law and protection. In 1839 the British government sent Captain William Hobson to administer the islands, impose law and order, and safeguard Maori interests. The British wanted good relations with the Maori for peaceful, law-abiding trade and settlement in the resource-rich country. They also had humanitarian (concern for human well-being) interests in creating a fair society.

At Waitangi in 1840, Hobson offered Maori leaders a proposal to bring New Zealand into the British Empire (an empire that controlled about 25 percent of the world in the nineteenth and early twentieth century). Under this agreement, in return for granting Britain authority over the islands, the Maori would receive clear possession of their remaining lands and full status as British citizens. In addition, the Maori would sell land only to the British government.

Hobson and other British officials believed the document would promote a fair society and protect the Maori from being cheated in land deals. After a day of discussion, most Maori leaders who were present—many were not present—decided to accept the terms, and they signed the Treaty of Waitangi on February 6, 1840. The treaty had been translated quickly and poorly into Maori. Few Maori understood its full meaning and how much they were ceding (giving up).

The agreement made New Zealand a British colony. Hobson moved the capital from Kororareka to the south side of Waitemata Harbor. The new capital, Auckland, soon became a trading center. The New Zealand Company established settlements in Wellington and Wanganui in 1840 and in New Plymouth and Nelson in 1842. The company also later founded Dunedin and Christchurch.

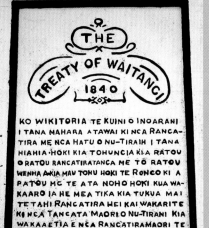

Farms and towns developed more rapidly on the South Island, where the Canterbury Plains provided treeless, fertile land for raising sheep and crops. Life for early settlers was challenging. Hard physical labor, illness, and poor housing were harsh realities. An unfamiliar and unpredictable land and climate caused great hardship to settlers used to European seasons. Manufactured goods and supplies had to be shipped across oceans and were hard to get and very expensive. Settlers learned to make do and rely on their native skills and on each other. Social classes that were separate in Europe mingled together, and people could raise their class standing in the new society as they could not in Europe. Servants could become landowners, for instance. Men and women used to performing separate duties found themselves working at all manner of chores. Men cooked meals and helped women give birth to babies, and women ran shops and cut timber. Children worked hard too, and their labor was often vital for the survival of a family.

Two obstacles discouraged many early immigrants from making their homes on the North Island. One was the thick forest that had to be cleared for farming. The second was the presence of strong Maori clans that showed growing resistance to parting with their land.

A few years after signing the Treaty of Waitangi, some Maori leaders began to reconsider the agreement. They realized that they could no longer sell land to private individuals but only to the government. They also saw Europeans reselling property for many times the original price as more and more settlers arrived. Many Maori chiefs who had never signed the treaty objected to selling their land at all.

In addition, as Auckland expanded, it replaced the Bay of Islands as a center of trade, which hurt the Maori economy. In the mid-1840s, the powerful Maori leader Hone Heke led uprisings in the area north of Auckland to protest unfair treatment by the Pakeha. After a year of fighting, the colonial troops of Governor George Grey—who replaced Hobson in 1845—defeated the rebels.

In 1852 Grey drafted laws that made New Zealand largely self-governing. The national parliament (lawmaking body), which first met in 1854, consisted of the Legislative Council, with members appointed by the governor-general (governor of a large territory), and the elected House of Representatives. Only male European landowners could vote for representatives.

◉ The Land Wars

In 1855 the Maori were still the largest population in the colony. They grew most of the food supply and controlled coastal shipping. Many Maori worked building roads and houses. Because of mission schools and government programs, some Maori could read and write.

Within just a few years, however, the Pakeha outnumbered the Maori. The number of Pakeha settlers grew to 59,000 by 1858, while the Maori population fell to 56,000. The continuing stream of immigrants alarmed many Maori. Some Maori groups on the North Island decided that the best way to protect their territory would be to unite under one leader. In 1858 they chose the Waikato chief Potatau Te Wherowhero as their king. They declared their lands tapu and placed them under the king's protection.

Governor Gore Browne, Grey's successor, considered the election of a Maori king illegal. He also decided that the colonists and the Maori would have to settle their differences by force. A dispute over land in Taranaki in 1860 became violent and triggered a series of confrontations between some Maori groups and the British—the Land Wars (1860–1872).

The British had difficulty subduing the Maori resisters because the Maori knew the terrain and were skilled warriors. Eventually, however, disease and the greater military strength of the British forces weakened the Maori fighters. They withdrew to King Country, between the Taranaki and Waikato regions. During the conflicts, the government seized about three million acres (1,214,034 hectares) of Maori land. Half was sold to help pay the cost of the battles. The other half was later returned to the Maori, but they had lost most of their best lands.

Economic Changes

To be closer to the more populated South Island, the government moved the capital from Auckland to Wellington—on the southern tip of the North Island—in 1865. Meanwhile, prospectors had discovered gold on the South Island. The find caused an economic boom that drew many immigrants to the country. But the gold dwindled in the second half of the decade, leaving thousands of people with no work. The cost of fighting the Land Wars added to New Zealand's hardships. And when prices for its main exports—wool from its vast sheep ranches and wheat—fell in the late 1860s, the country faced serious economic problems.

In 1870 New Zealand's treasurer, Julius Vogel, proposed a solution to these problems through a program to create jobs and develop the country at the same time. The government borrowed $40 million to construct railways, roads, bridges, telegraph lines, and government buildings. Railroads opened interior areas of the North Island, and settlers cleared hillsides for agriculture. Trains carried meat, wool, grain, and dairy products to ports for shipment on new steamship lines.

The transportation networks simplified travel within the country and aided the development of manufacturing. Factories produced woolen cloth, farm machinery, and refrigeration and mining equipment. By paying low wages, New Zealand's manufacturers could sell their goods abroad despite the high cost of shipping to distant places. By the end of the 1870s, the white population had grown to about 500,000.

Freezing and refrigeration came into use on ships during the 1880s. The first cargo of frozen meat sent to Great Britain in 1882 earned a considerable profit for New Zealand farmers. The success of this technology made them less dependent on wool and wheat for income.

Social Reforms

Despite improvements in transportation and manufacturing, however, New Zealand experienced severe economic problems throughout the 1880s. Prices for wool and grain exports remained low. Unemployed farmworkers could not find jobs in factories. Thousands of immigrants who had come during the gold rush left New Zealand.

As poverty spread, unemployed workers demanded legislation that would improve living conditions. Many New Zealanders wanted the government to provide land for more farms. Others called for laws to protect workers, including women and children, from long working hours and unsafe conditions in factories and shops.

The newly formed Liberal Party won a majority of House seats in 1890 and responded to these demands. The Liberals enacted sweeping social reforms. The government created more than five thousand new farms, mostly on land bought from the Maori. It passed the Land and Income Tax Act, which forced many wealthy property owners to sell parts of their estates to pay their taxes.

New laws gave employees the right to negotiate with employers and better working conditions. In 1893 New Zealand became the first nation in the world to give voting rights to women. That same year, the government extended free education from the primary to the secondary level. In 1898 the country passed a plan to provide pensions (payments) to the elderly. By the turn of the century, New Zealanders benefited from some of the world's most advanced social programs.

In 1907 Britain granted the colony status as a dominion—a self-governing country within the British Empire. When World War I broke out in 1914, New Zealand sided with Britain against Germany. The dominion sent more than 100,000 troops to Europe and Africa. They were called Anzacs because they fought in the Australian and New Zealand Army Corps (ANZAC). By the war's end in 1918, 17,000 New Zealanders had died as a result of the fighting, and many more were wounded. The worst loss of life took place during a major but poorly planned battle at Gallipoli, Turkey.

WHY WOMEN SHOULD GET THE VOTE, 1888

Kate Sheppard was a leader who fought for equal rights for women, including the right to vote. In the 1888 pamphlet "Ten Reasons Why the Women of N.Z. Should Vote," she wrote that women should be allowed to vote alongside men, "because it has not yet been proved that the intelligence of women is only equal to that of children, nor that their intelligence is on a par with that of lunatics or criminals." (Children, the mentally ill, and criminals did not have the right to vote.) New Zealand women won the right to vote in 1893.

The 1930s and 1940s

After World War I and throughout the 1920s, New Zealand developed its agriculture and industry, and living conditions continued to improve. In the 1930s, however, New Zealand's economy suffered from the effects of a worldwide economic depression (job loss and business failure). Prices for agricultural exports dropped, and thousands of people lost their jobs. Those lucky enough to keep their jobs had to take pay cuts. In addition, the nation could not afford to maintain many of its social programs, so it reduced spending on health services, pension, education, and public works, such as roads and sanitation.

In 1935 the Labor Party came to power and began to increase spending to create jobs. It also set up a broad government insurance system. This program included increased pension coverage for the elderly, the disabled, widows, and orphans. It also paid most medical costs for citizens.

The government guaranteed farmers minimum prices for their products and built houses for workers. It cut the workweek from forty-four to forty hours. From 1936 through the next decade, the Labor Party strengthened New Zealand as a welfare state—a country in which the government takes responsibility for the well-being of its citizens.

As part of its economic recovery, New Zealand became less dependent on Great Britain by developing more industries and by establishing its own unit of money and a central bank. Nevertheless, when Britain declared war on Germany and its allies in 1939, New Zealand quickly did the same. About 140,000 New Zealand soldiers served with British and Allied troops during World War II (1939–1945). Many battles were in the Pacific region, not far from New Zealand. More than 11,800 New Zealanders lost their lives in the conflict against Germany, Italy, and Japan, and an additional 15,700 suffered injuries.

The wartime battles in Asia helped New Zealanders realize that their country's past ties to Britain could not guarantee their security in the South Pacific, so far away from Britain. As a result, in 1944 New Zealand signed the Canberra Pact to strength relations with much closer Australia. New Zealand also formed a strong alliance with the United States, which had used the country as a base of operations against Japan during the war. After the war, New Zealand joined the United Nations (UN), an international organization that works for peace and cooperation among nations, as a founding member.

To learn more about the Anzacs and New Zealand's involvement in World War I and World War II, visit www.vgsbooks.com for links.

Postwar Developments

The British Empire had been greatly weakened by World War II, and many of its colonies gained independence after the war. New Zealand formally gained full independence from Great Britain in 1947 under the Statute of Westminster. The new nation became a member of the British Commonwealth (an organization that includes Britain and its former colonies). New Zealand also entered into two defense agreements. The ANZUS Treaty (with Australia and the United States) and the Southeast Asia Treaty Organization (SEATO) both sought to maintain peace in the South Pacific. New Zealand troops served with UN forces in the Korean War (1950–1953).

Along with responsibilities in international affairs, New Zealand was faced with domestic changes and concerns. A postwar economic boom expanded industrial production and created new jobs. Many Maori, Pakeha, and Pacific Islanders moved to the thriving Auckland area to work.

In 1951 the Maori Women's Welfare League was formed. Whina Cooper, the first president of the league, led this influential group of Maori women. It brought education, health, housing, and childhood needs to government attention and pushed for political changes. One of the league's successes was the establishment of play centers for young children throughout the country. The group also resisted the continuing assimilation of Maori culture into the Pakeha mainstream and called for the establishment of a diverse, multicultural society.

In the 1960s, New Zealand again sent troops into war, serving with U.S. troops in the Vietnam War (1957–1975). This controversial decision sparked public debate. Many young people became politically active in antiwar causes and in promoting social causes such as woman's rights, civil liberties, and racial equality. Environmentalists began to promote conservation of natural resources. These activists opposed both nuclear testing and the admission of nuclear-equipped ships into New Zealand ports.

By 1972 the National Party had held power and run the government, except for one three-year period, since 1949. In 1972 the Labor Party won a majority of seats in the House of Representatives. But the country soon faced an economic crisis.

◉ Hard Times

In 1973 Britain—New Zealand's main trading partner—joined the European Community (EC, the forerunner of the European Union). This organization required Britain to limit purchases of agricultural goods produced outside the EC. As a result, Britain sharply cut imports from New Zealand, and many New Zealanders lost their jobs. Adding to the economic crisis were rising prices for oil and other imported goods.

As conditions worsened, voters in 1975 again elected the National Party. Under the leadership of Robert Muldoon, the government tightened controls on wages, prices, immigration, and imports. Muldoon also increased public borrowing and spending—a method that had helped New Zealand recover from past crises. This time, however, the strategy failed and economic problems grew.

Muldoon's administration also had to deal with tensions between the Maori and Pakeha populations. Maori activists began to work for the preservation of their culture. They began to demand social rights that had been denied to them, such as the use of their language in education. Under the terms of the Treaty of Waitangi, they also sought the return of land and water resources that had been taken illegally from them. In 1975 Whina Cooper led a Maori Land March from the far north to the steps of parliament in Wellington, calling for justice in long-standing land claims. Tens of thousands of people had joined the march by the end of its eight-month trek. That year, the Treaty of Waitangi Act set up the Waitangi Tribunal (court) to investigate Maori land claims.

Although the National Party won the elections of 1978 and 1981, voter support declined. As New Zealand's economic troubles persisted, the Labor Party gained a majority of seats in the House of Representatives, and David Lange became prime minister.

Lange strengthened New Zealand's opposition to nuclear weapons. His government decided that such weapons, as well as ships powered by nuclear fuel, could not enter New Zealand's waters. This policy prevented U.S. military vessels from stopping in New Zealand. In response, the United States announced it would no longer guarantee New Zealand's security under the ANZUS Treaty.

Lange's government, under the leadership of finance minister Roger Douglas, also began an aggressive economic reform program to improve the economy and to lower the high rate of inflation (rising prices). The government cut income taxes and placed a large sales tax on goods and serv-

THE RAINBOW WARRIOR

In 1985 New Zealand opposition to French nuclear testing in the South Pacific resulted in tragedy. Greenpeace is an international organization that works to protect the environment. One of its ships, the Rainbow Warrior, was anchored in the harbor at Auckland, ready to sail north toward French Polynesia to protest against French nuclear testing there. French secret service agents blew up and sunk the ship in the harbor. The ship's Greenpeace photographer, Fernando Pereira, was killed in the explosion. Ten years later, in 1995, a new Rainbow Warrior set sail to protest continued French nuclear testing in the Pacific.

ices. It also cut spending on national programs for social services, including health care.

Government also reduced its involvement in business in an effort to help the economy function better. The government began to encourage free enterprise (business that is not controlled by the government) by lifting controls on wages, prices, and interest rates. It stopped giving farmers subsidies (payments to keep income at a certain level). Tariffs (taxes on imports) that had protected New Zealand manufacturers from foreign competition were also reduced or eliminated on most products. These dramatic economic changes were referred to as Rogernomics, after Roger Douglas.

As the economy adjusted to these changes, however, unemployment increased and hundreds of farmers lost their land. Industrial expansion slowed almost to a standstill. By the end of 1988, unemployment was very high at 11 percent. In August 1989, Lange resigned as head of the government.

Late Twentieth Century

After two short-term governments, the National Party was elected again in 1990 and 1993, with Jim Bolger as prime minister. His popularity grew with the country's economic growth and with his 1995 stand against France's nuclear weapons testing in the South Pacific. The government also began settling land claims with the Maori by awarding them money and land and issuing a formal apology for previous injustices toward the indigenous people.

In 1996 New Zealand adopted proportional representation in the government, designed to increase the role of smaller parties in government. Under this system, political parties that win the largest proportion of votes get the most number of seats in parliament. They then form coalitions (combine to share power) with parties that win a smaller proportion of votes so that these minority points of view are also represented.

In 1997 the struggling National Party appointed the nation's first female prime minister, Jennifer Shipley. Her government also struggled with another economic recession. In 1999 New Zealand troops joined a UN peacekeeping force in the island nation of East Timor. Economic downturns led to another change of government in 1999, when Labor leader Helen Clark became prime minister.

The Twenty-First Century

In the early twenty-first century, New Zealand's economy grew at a rate of about 3 percent, a relatively good growth. Unemployment dropped from almost 8 percent in 1999 to 5.3 percent in 2002.

WOMEN LEADERS

In 2001 Silvia Cartwright was appointed to the office of governor-general. With her appointment, women filled five important public roles in New Zealand. The prime minister, leader of the opposition party, attorney general, chief justice, and governor-general were all women in 2005. The chief of state of New Zealand (a symbolic position) is also a woman, Queen Elizabeth II of Great Britain. And the role of monarch of the Waikato Maori tribes (a confederation of four major tribes) had been filled by a woman for the first time when Princess Piki became the Maori queen in 1966. Her official title is Te Arikinui Dame Te Atairangikaahu.

Helen Clark was elected as New Zealand's prime minister in 1999. She has been a member of the Labor Party since 1971 and has held office at every level of her party. Like many other Kiwis, Clark is an avid hiker and mountain climber. To learn more about the prime minister and New Zealand's government, visit www.vgsbooks.com for links.

The Labor-led coalition government increased spending on health and education. New Zealand also saw a rise in its film and tourism industries due to the worldwide success of the *Lord of the Rings* movies, made in New Zealand and featuring its astonishing landscapes. In July 2002, the Labor Party won a majority of seats in parliament with 41 percent of the votes, and Helen Clark remained prime minister. She continues to aggressively pursue trade opportunities for New Zealand in the global market.

New Zealand takes an active role in peacekeeping in the Pacific region. In 2003 it sent troops, along with other nations, to restore order in the troubled Solomon Islands in the South Pacific. New Zealand is also an active member in the global efforts against terrorism and sent troops to Afghanistan to help remove the terrorist group al-Qaeda, which is based there. However, the Labor-led government opposed the 2003 U.S.-led invasion of Iraq to remove the government of dictator Saddam Hussein.

New Zealand society continues to value a healthy society with equal rights for all. Two settlements of Treaty of Waitangi Act land claims in 2004 gave millions of dollars to Maori groups to buy back their own land from the government. In December 2004, a law banned smoking in bars, restaurants, and workplaces. That same month, a civil union law was passed, giving legal recognition to same-sex partnerships.

In 2005 a devastating tsunami (tidal wave) hit southeast Asia. New Zealand was one of the first countries on the scene with aid.

Government

New Zealand is an independent nation in the commonwealth of former British dependencies. Its parliamentary system of government is closely patterned after Britain's. Its constitution is not one written document but a series of laws passed by parliament and important rulings by the courts. The governor-general—a mostly ceremonial role (limited in authority)—represents the British monarch, the formal head of state and symbolic ruler of New Zealand.

Executive authority rests with the prime minister and the cabinet (a group of advisers) of usually about twenty members. The prime minister is the leader of the party that holds the most seats in the House of Representatives, or parliament. The leading party forms a coalition with parties that have fewer seats in the parliament.

Legislative authority lies with the unicameral (one house) House of Representatives. It has 120 members. Citizens vote directly to elect 69 members of parliament, including 7 seats reserved for Maori representatives. Members serve three-year terms. All citizens eighteen years of age or older must become registered voters, and voter turnout during elections is very high. Parliamentary elections normally occur every three years, although the prime minister can call an election sooner if the House does not agree with the administration on a major issue.

The highest judicial (legal) body in New Zealand is the Court of Appeals. Decisions of that court are final unless parties obtain permission to take their cases to Great Britain's Privy Council. Cases reach the top court from a lower appeals court called the High Court. The High Court deals with major crimes, appeals, and civil claims. The nation's principal trial courts are the district courts, which serve specific regions. Some courts have special functions, including family court, environment court, and Maori Land Court.

The country is divided into sixteen administrative regions. More than one hundred county governments provide for the needs of rural populations. Governmental units in cities and towns handle local matters. Because it is small in area, New Zealand has been able to develop a strong central government with most of the responsibility for running the country resting with government officials in Wellington.

THE PEOPLE

With an average of 38 people per square mile (15 people per sq. km),
New Zealand is a lightly populated country, compared to an average of
61 people per square mile (24 people per sq. km) in the rest of the
developed world (other countries with well-developed industry and a
high standard of living). Family farms and small towns of up to 10,000
people dot the countryside. Despite New Zealand's strong rural economy, however, close to 80 percent of the country's population lives in
cities. About three-fourths of New Zealand's 4 million people, including most Maori, live on the North Island, mainly in urban areas on the
coasts and lower hills. Auckland, with a population of 1.2 million,
hosts about 25 percent of the entire population.

   Many young, well-educated people emigrate (leave their homeland)
from New Zealand to find jobs in more prosperous Australia. The population still increases every year, however, because of a sufficiently
high birthrate of 14 births per 1,000 people every year, an average of 2
children per woman. A steady flow of immigrants, mostly Pacific

Islanders and Asians, also contributes to overall population growth. Emigration reduces the growth rate, however, which was less than 1 percent in the early 2000s. At that slow level of expansion, the population will be 5,100,000 in 2050.

◉ Daily Life

New Zealanders share their land with almost 50 million sheep, but only a small number of people live on large sheep stations (ranches). On small farms, mechanization has decreased the need for workers. As a result, farming employs only 9.5 percent of the total labor force. Most New Zealanders hold jobs in manufacturing, commerce, the service sector, communications, and construction. They work a five-day, forty-hour week. Most businesses close on weekends.

The majority of the country's citizens enjoy a comfortable standard of living, although in times of economic hardship, some families live in poverty. Government services assist low-income New Zealanders.

Public housing is available for low-income people, and there are almost no homeless people in New Zealand. Most people live much like modest, middle-class people in the United States or Europe. New Zealanders value hard work, social equality, and self-reliance. Most families own an automobile and their own small home. Gardening is very popular, and people are proud of their gardens. Rivers, lakes, seacoasts, and mountains provide many recreational opportunities within easy reach of most people.

◉ Ethnic Mixture

Persons of European descent make up 79 percent of New Zealand's population. Maori make up 10 percent of the population. Intermarriage between Maori and Pakeha is and has been common, and most people who consider themselves Maori are at least partly Pakeha. Pacific Islanders make up 4 percent. Included in the remaining 7 percent of the nation's residents are people with Chinese, East Indian, and Southeast Asian backgrounds. New Zealand's Maori and Pacific Islander populations are growing most rapidly, both groups having more youthful populations, with a median age of 22. The median age of people with European ancestry is 37.

About 90 percent of New Zealanders with European ancestry trace their family origins to Great Britain. The early British immigrants adopted an attitude of equality in social matters and favored a community approach to solving problems. This British heritage is shared by most New Zealanders and is reflected in their customs, family ties, and language.

Many New Zealanders of **European ancestry** engage in British customs. This couple enjoys afternoon tea, a favorite British tradition, along Auckland's waterfront. To learn more about New Zealand's people, visit www.vgsbooks.com for links.

The strong link to Great Britain has influenced the course of New Zealand's history. Ties with Britain have loosened, but the relative isolation of New Zealand has led the country to keep many British cultural values unchanged. As Great Britain has rapidly changed with huge influxes of immigrants after World War II, there is a saying that New Zealanders are more British than the British. Many neighborhoods still look very British, with tidy gardens and plain houses. The main urban areas, however, reflect the influence of Maori, Asian, and North American cultures on New Zealand's way of life.

Non-Maori Pacific Islanders began immigrating to New Zealand in the mid-1800s, when missionaries brought them to the country for religious training. After World War II, the rate of this migration—mostly from Western Samoa and the Cook Islands—increased. The Pacific Islanders do not all share the same culture and language. Some groups have chosen to preserve their customs and pass them on to their children. Some Pacific Islanders have struggled against discrimination in housing and job opportunities. Many have had to accept low-paying jobs. Others have achieved considerable economic success.

◉ The Maori

After World War II, the Maori began moving from rural areas to urban centers—particularly Auckland—to find jobs, and 90 percent of the Maori lived in cities by the 1980s. The change in lifestyle caused problems for many Maori, who had been accustomed to living with extended families in close-knit communities. Because their rural schools had prepared the Maori for an agricultural way of life, most of them lacked the broad educational background needed to obtain good jobs. Some Pakeha property owners refused to rent to Maori tenants. Social problem such as unemployment, poverty, and poor health care made urban living difficult. Urban youth began to form gangs that replaced absent family groups, and gang violence increased. In the 1970s, a Maori social protest movement began. It worked to bring the challenges of the Maori to public attention. It also called for a renewal of Maoritanga, or Maori culture. One of the results was that Maori became an official language of New Zealand in 1987.

In the 1990s, young Maori led a huge revival of interest in Maoritanga. Some Maori who spoke only English began to learn Maori. Schools began to teach the Maori language. At special centers, young and old study the traditional arts of their people—weaving, carving, singing, dancing, and storytelling.

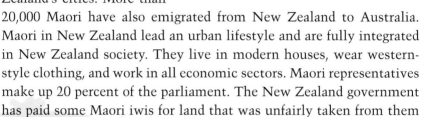

A Maori woman strips flax for use in weaving at the Maori Arts & Crafts Institute in Rotorua. Many Maori are expressing a renewed interest in Maoritanga and attending such institutes to learn the **traditional arts and crafts** of their ancestors.

In the twenty-first century, 75 percent of the 400,000 Maori live in New Zealand's cities. More than 20,000 Maori have also emigrated from New Zealand to Australia. Maori in New Zealand lead an urban lifestyle and are fully integrated in New Zealand society. They live in modern houses, wear western-style clothing, and work in all economic sectors. Maori representatives make up 20 percent of the parliament. The New Zealand government has paid some Maori iwis for land that was unfairly taken from them in colonial times. Many iwis have invested their money in businesses that provide work for their people. Farming and tourism-related businesses have been especially successful. But the Maori, who have lower incomes and a shorter life expectancy than Pakeha, also have a much higher rate of unemployment. Maori people are three times more likely to be unemployed than non-Maori.

Some rural Maori maintain traditional community life that centers on the *marae*. Social, political, and ceremonial events take place in this open area of land with a community building, a *whare*, for eating and sleeping. Urban Maori return to their ancestral marae on special occasions, such as weddings and funerals.

ONE BIG MOUTHFUL

Maori words can be amazingly long because many words may be strung together to form one word. The supposedly longest place name in the world is a Maori name for a place on the East Coast: Taumatawhakatangihangakoauauotamateaturipukakapikimaungahoronukupokaiwhenuakitanatahu. It means "The place where Tamatea, the man with the big knees, who slid, climbed, and swallowed mountains, known as landeater, played his flute to his loved one."

Others attend marae meetinghouses in cities. These new, urban marae have successfully adapted traditional ways to modern circumstances.

Language

Maori language and literature was unwritten until the arrival of Europeans. Maori stories, songs, legends, and history were passed down through the generations. British missionaries began to teach English to the Maori. They also wrote down Maori language. English-style schools began teaching Maori children the English language, and teachers refused to let students speak Maori. By the late 1880s, many Maori children grew up unable to speak their own language. Because the British dominated New Zealand society, Maori people thought that learning English was necessary to their success. By the 1980s, Maori was in danger of completely dying out.

The Maori Language Act of 1987 established Maori as an official language alongside English. Virtually all Maori speak English, and about 33 percent of them also speak Maori. Maori is part of the Polynesian language family, along with the native languages spoken in other South Pacific islands, including Tahiti, Hawaii, and Samoa. Samoan is the only other non-English language that is spoken by a significant number of people in New Zealand. Maori words can be very long in written form, but the language is actually fairly easy for nonnative speakers to pronounce.

Health Care

New Zealand has a history of providing health care for all its citizens. The idea of community responsibility for social welfare (well-being) for everybody is a long-held value among the country's citizens. As a

NEW ZEALAND ENGLISH

New Zealanders use many words and phrases that are not familiar to American speakers of English. Here are a few of them:

bach: a small cabin used for vacations, usually on a beach
barbie: barbecue, a very popular activity
cockies: farmers, including sheep-cocky and cow-cocky (dairy farmer)
Enzed: New Zealand, from the initials "NZ" (Z is pronounced "zed")
fly cemetery: a small tart with raisins in it
long drop: an outside toilet
mate: good friend
the other side: Australia
rellies: relatives
scrubber: small child
she'll be right: everything will be all right, don't worry
station: a large farm
tall poppy: someone who has too high an opinion of his or herself
tramping: hiking

THE HEALING TEA TREE

The Maori people have long used different parts of the manuka plant, which grows up to 35 feet (11 m) tall, as medicine. Captain James Cook dubbed the tall plant the tea tree because tea brewed from its leaves treated all kinds of ailments, including sore throats and eye diseases. The trees give off a sweet smell, but the tea's strong flavor is not pleasant to the taste. New Zealand scientists are studying the plant's antibiotic (germ-killing) properties.

welfare state for most of the twentieth century, New Zealand provided benefits and services to help its people maintain an adequate standard of living. The government paid money to families or individuals who were unable to support themselves because of sickness, accident, unemployment, disability, old age, or single parenthood. Free or low-cost public health care was available to all.

The welfare state was very expensive. In the late twentieth century, the government cut back its control of social services in an effort to improve the economy. Some of the national health care sector was privatized, or sold to private owners. Government spending on social services was reduced. Some rural hospitals were closed. People with the lowest incomes, which includes a higher proportion of Maori and Pacific Islanders than Pakeha, were hardest hit. With loss of free health and social service resources, there was an increase in rates of teenage pregnancy, alcoholism, and drug use in poor communities. In the twenty-first century, New Zealand still has an excellent health care system, though it is relatively expensive.

New Zealand's high-quality health care system is reflected in a high life expectancy of 78 years of age (76 years for men and 81 years for women). The average life expectancy for developed countries around the world is 76 years. New Zealand's infant mortality rate is 5.6 per 1,000 births, again a better average than most developed countries, which average 7 infant deaths per 1,000 births. Women in New Zealand have an average of 2 children each. Abortion is legal, and contraceptive (birth control) use is high.

The prevalence (rate of infection) of HIV/AIDS (human immunodeficiency virus/acquired immunodeficiency syndrome) among adults aged 15 to 49 years is 0.1 percent in New Zealand, among the lowest in the world. The United Nations estimates the worldwide prevalence of HIV/AIDS is 1.1 percent of the adult population, a total of about 38 million people around the globe. New Zealand's ample public health information about the deadly and incurable disease—which is spread by infected body fluids during sex or through needles that have been con-

Children learn the **Maori language** at a school in Waima. Maori became an official language of New Zealand in 1987.

taminated with infected blood—keeps the infection rate low. The use of condoms, which reduces body fluid contamination during sex, helps prevent the spread of HIV/AIDS.

▶ Education

Education has been a strongly held value in New Zealand since colonial times. New Zealand has a 99 percent literacy rate, which means that virtually all New Zealanders can read and write. Education is free from the ages of 5 through 19. Attendance is required for ages 6 through 16, and the school attendance rate is 100 percent. Many children 3 to 5 years of age attend play centers, partially funded by the government. Students who live in remote areas can take correspondence courses that are broadcast over radio stations. Secondary school graduates who pass a national examination can attend one of six universities, whose total enrollment is nearly 50,000 students. Community colleges, technical institutes, and an agricultural college provide additional educational opportunities. Many New Zealanders take advantage of continuing and adult education programs for lifelong learning.

LANGUAGE NESTS

The study and teaching of Maoritanga has been revived at all levels in New Zealand, starting with very young children. The Maori language was in danger of disappearing altogether by the 1980s. Concerned Maori leaders established five "language nests," or schools, called Te Kohanga Reo in Maori, to teach their language and culture to preschool Maori children. (Pakeha are welcome too.) Soon more than eight hundred language nests opened. Pacific Islanders have also developed similar early childhood programs to teach their native languages. Primary and secondary schools have developed bilingual programs to teach in both English and Maori. In "total immersion" schools, Maori is the only language spoken.

CULTURAL LIFE

New Zealand's cultural life was largely shaped by European, particularly British, elements, and the Maori and other non-European groups were pressured to assimilate (join the dominant culture). But Maori traditions have added to the culture, especially since the 1970s, when there was a renaissance (rebirth) of Maoritanga. Pacific Islanders, including Samoans and Tongans, and immigrants from Asia have also influenced cultural traditions with their rich heritage.

New Zealand's government has encouraged a flourishing arts community. The New Zealand Literary Fund supports writers and publishers. The Queen Elizabeth II Arts Council provides government-funded support for theater, music, and dance companies.

Many New Zealanders, inspired by their beautiful country and supportive society, become artists. Many art forms are represented in the country, including painting, pottery, sculpture, glassware, spinning, weaving, and wood carving. Music, theater, ballet, modern dance, literature, filmmaking, and architecture are also well repre-

sented. Sports and outdoor recreation are very popular in this country that has such beautiful and unspoiled wilderness.

Maori Religious Culture

Before the Europeans came, Maori religion was complex and fully integrated into all parts of life. It was believed that *mauri* (life force) and *wairua* (spirit) resided in all things. The Maori were polytheistic (worshiped many gods). Rangi was the Sky Father and Papa was the Earth Mother, and there were many other gods of forests, mountains, war, agriculture, and so forth. Tapu was a central idea in Maori belief and society. If some thing or some action was considered to have the presence of supernatural power, it was called tapu, or sacred, and required special caution. The Maori believed that breaking tapu angered the gods, who could cause people harm, such as sickness and accidents. In order to keep the gods happy, people believed that everyday actions had to be carried out properly. Priests could communicate with the gods and perform the essential rituals and offerings. They also were the keepers of the family and group history, the songs and stories of the iwi.

The Maori also placed great importance on *mana*, or respectability, which was considered a supernatural quality. In modern times, mana is more often considered a reflection of personal achievements. The importance of balance and fairness between people, and an individual's personal composure and self-respect, were also strongly held Maori beliefs. Though most Maori converted to Christianity in the 1800s, the concepts of sacredness, honor, balance, and composure remain qualities that are still highly valued in Maori culture.

Religion Fast Fact: The English word *taboo*, meaning something forbidden for supernatural or cultural reasons, comes from the Maori word *tapu*.

Religions and Holidays

In modern times, most Pakeha and Maori belong to the Christian faith. The leading Christian congregations in the country are Anglican (Church of England, with 24 percent of the population), Presbyterian (18 percent), Roman Catholic (15 percent), and Methodist and other Protestants (10 percent). Maori forms of Christianity, including Ratana, which was started in 1918 by a Maori religious leader named Tahupotiki Ratana, are still practiced too. Only about 11 percent of the population regularly attends worship services. Small numbers of other world religions, including Buddhists, Hindus, Muslims, and Jews, are also represented in New Zealand. About 33 percent of the population does not belong to any religion. New Zealand culture is largely secular (nonreligious). Churches do not

The foundation of Christchurch's **Anglican cathedral** was laid in 1864, but the cathedral wasn't actually completed until 1904. It is the most famous and most visited cathedral in New Zealand.

A man plays the bagpipes during the annual **Waitangi Day** celebration. Waitangi Day has been celebrated in New Zealand since 1932.

exert a great influence in New Zealand, and religious matters are strictly separated from the state.

Public holidays in New Zealand include New Year's Day and the day after (January 1 and 2); Waitangi Day, or New Zealand Day, commemorating the signing of the Treaty of Waitangi (February 6); Good Friday and Easter Monday (variable dates in March, April, or May); ANZAC Day, honoring New Zealand's military (April 25); the Queen's Birthday, in honor of Queen Elizabeth II of Great Britain (the first Monday in June); Labor Day (the fourth Monday in October); and Christmas and Boxing Day (December 25 and 26). Boxing Day is so named because servants used to receive boxes of presents from their employers on the day after Christmas.

◉ Art

During centuries of isolation from other peoples, the Maori applied their artistic talent to the wood, stones, flax, and other materials of New Zealand, developing unique art forms and intricate designs. Carving was the art of men, and weaving was the art of women. Both forms decorated meetinghouses and the homes of important people, as well as everyday items. Artists also decorated giant war canoes with beautiful, bold carvings. Carved wooden figures of ancestors and mythic figures were also part of the whare (meetinghouses). Besides wood carving, the Maori also carved greenstone (jade) into ornaments and meres (war clubs).

MAORI TATTOOS

Moko, or facial tattooing, is one of the most famous and visible of Maori art forms. Traditionally, moko served to mark rites of passages, such as reaching marriageable age, and to celebrate achievements. Young men would be given simple designs and would win the right to more ornate spiral patterns by doing well in warfare. Eventually a man could earn a full facial tattoo (above), a sign of status. Women's moko were simpler in design and usually were applied only on their lips and chins. The moko were created by an expert, who used a sharp bird-bone chisel to etch the design into the face and then filled the lines in with ink made of ash and fat. Some modern Maori still practice traditional moko, but mostly people use face paint to apply temporary tattoos for special occasions.

Modern Maori carry on the artistic traditions of their people. The New Zealand Maori Arts and Crafts Institute in Rotorua, established in 1963, is the main training institution for the traditional arts. Master carver Paaki Harrison and his wife, Hinemoa, organized the creation of a traditional *whare whakairo* (carved meetinghouse) at the University of Auckland.

In the 1950s, some Maori artists began to mix traditional Maori imagery and materials into the traditions of European art. This movement of artists is called the Maori Renaissance. Maori women artists began to express their separate artistic identities under the name *mana wahine* (women's dignity). Robyn Kahukiwa, drawing on her experience as a Maori woman and a mother, painted a series of strong women from Maori mythology. Artists continue to blend their own ideas with old styles, creating new Maori art. One of New Zealand's most important and innovative artists, painter Ralph Hotere, for instance, collaborates with poets and writers designing banners for libraries and other works. Modern Maori artists are featured in many galleries and museums around the country and the world.

New Zealand has many highly acclaimed Pakeha painters too. Charles Heaphy, a soldier and surveyor who arrived in New Zealand in 1840, became the country's first great painter. Frances Hodgkins (1869–1947), one of New Zealand's most famous painters, left her homeland in 1913 when she was forty-four. She went to London, where she first won recognition for her figurative (realistic) paintings. Colin McCahon (1919–1987), the nation's most famous and influential artist, painted landscapes that reflected his own visions. Peter McIntyre's landscapes realistically portray the New Zealand countryside and are very popular. Gordon Walters uses the coiled shape of a young fern leaf, which also inspired Maori carvers, as a dominant design in his abstract paintings.

Literature

New Zealand authors produce world-famous literature. In the early 1900s, some Pakeha writers traveled to Europe to work. Among these was Katherine Mansfield (1888–1923), New Zealand's most famous literary figure. She began publishing her innovative short stories after moving to Britain in 1906 at the age of nineteen. Two of her most widely read short stories are "At the Bay" and "Prelude." Both stories are loving tributes to her New Zealand childhood. Mystery writer Ngaio Marsh (1895–1982) lived most of her life in Christchurch, New Zealand. Her well-known mystery novels feature British detective Roderick Alleyn.

Katherine Mansfield lived a bold, socially unconventional life. She wrote in her journal what was to become a famous quote, "Risk, risk anything! Care no more for the opinions of others, for those voices. Do the hardest thing on earth for you. Act for yourself. Face the truth."

In the 1930s, works reflecting New Zealand's own distinctive culture began to emerge. Leading this movement were some Pakeha poets— A. R. D. Fairburn, Robin Hyde, Allen Curnow, and James K. Baxter. Using his poetry to celebrate the wilderness and to express compassion for social issues such as alcoholism, Baxter lived the last part of his life in a Maori community. Many New Zealand authors have gained international success writing children's literature. Margaret Mahy has written more than one hundred novels for children and won the prestigious Carnegie Medal for *The Changeover* and *The Haunting*.

The popular writer Frank Sargeson (1903–1982) wrote many internationally acclaimed stories and novels about New Zealand but died in poverty near Auckland. He played a major role in the life of Janet Frame (1924–2004), one of New Zealand's greatest writers, by offering her support and a place to live while she wrote her first novel. This novel, *Owls Do Cry*, is about a woman in a mental institution, an experience Frame herself had undergone when she was wrongly diagnosed with schizophrenia (a severe mental illness) in her twenties. Frame's autobiography, *An Angel at My Table*, was made into a film by director Jane Campion in 1990. Maurice Shadbolt, known primarily for his fiction, has written several nonfiction accounts of New Zealand.

Traditional Maori literature was sung and told out loud. It was not written down until the 1800s, when the Europeans introduced writing. Maori writers came into view in the 1970s, expressing in English what it means to be Maori in Pakeha society. Patricia Grace (b. 1937) is known for her 1978 novel about a young Maori woman in love with a Pakeha, *Mutuwhenua: The moon sleeps*. Witi Ihimaera (b. 1944) published *Tangi* (*Lament*), a novel about father-son relationships, in 1973. His novel for young adults, *The Whale Rider*, about a Maori girl who has spiritual leadership abilities traditionally held by males, was made into a film in 2002. It was popular with both Maori and Pakeha. *The Bone People* by Keri Hulme (b. 1947) won Britain's top literary award—the Booker Prize—in 1985. In imaginative, poetic language, Hulme tells the story of three outcasts from society who find each other. After almost twenty years of literary silence, Hulme published *Stonefish* in 2004, a collection of short stories and poems. Alan Duff writes about the plight of a modern, urban Maori family in his novels *Once Were Warriors* (1992) and *What Becomes of the Broken-Hearted* (1997). *Once Were Warriors* was also made into a film. The poetry of Hone Tuwhare has won a worldwide following.

This still from the movie **Whale Rider** features Keisha Castle-Hughes, the youngest actress ever nominated for a Best Actress Academy Award. Hughes is of Australian and Maori descent.

New Zealand also has some important Pacific Islander authors. Albert Wendt is a Samoan novelist who has also published poetry and short stories. Niuean (from the tiny country of Niue) John Puhiatau Pule wrote *Burn My Head in Heaven* (1998) about the experience of Pacific Islanders in New Zealand. He is also an artist, taking a modern approach to traditional forms.

◑ Film and Media

New Zealand's film industry first produced notable film in the 1970s. *Sleeping Dogs* (1977) launched the film career of New Zealand actor Sam Neill. A landmark early Maori film, *Utu* (*Revenge*), was released in 1983. Lee Tamahori's violent film *Once Were Warriors* (1994), based on Alan Duff's novel, brought the Maori experiences of cultural alienation, urbanization, and renewal to international attention. *Footrot Flats* in 1986 starred New Zealand's favorite cartoon character, a sheepherding dog known as The Dog. Jane Campion, one of New Zealand's most famous film directors, adapted Janet Frame's *An Angel at My Table*. Originally made for New Zealand television, it became an international success as a film. Sam Neill starred in Campion's most famous film so far, *The Piano* (1994), a somber love story about early British settlers. It was filmed on the wild, rugged west coast of the North Island. Anna Paquin won Best Supporting Actress at the Academy Awards for her role in the film. Writer-director Peter Jackson has made several acclaimed films, including *Heavenly Creatures* (1992) about two schoolgirls who commit matricide (mother murder). Jackson brought New Zealand into new world notice with the huge international success of his film adaptation of J. R. R. Tolkien's trilogy, *The Lord of the Rings*. Filmed on 150 separate locations in New Zealand, the three films, released in the early 2000s, boosted New Zealand's reputation as a tourist destination and as a place to shoot films.

New Zealand does not have one national newspaper, but many daily newspapers cover world news. The country has hundreds of radio stations and dozens of television channels, including ones that broadcast in Maori. The government-run Broadcasting Corporation operates a radio station and two television channels. Some television programs produced in New Zealand have won international audiences. *Xena, Warrior Princess*, a TV show written, produced, and directed in New Zealand from 1995 to 2001, was popular all over the world.

◑ Music

Traditionally, Maori had songs for all occasions—songs of welcome, songs of love, songs of prayer, songs of war. Maori used song to express feelings and religious beliefs and to pass on history and myth. Song was accompanied with dance, and people would sing and dance for recreation as well as for ceremonial purposes. A special category of Maori music is *haka*, or action songs that are a kind of performance art or sign language with music. Performers use their bodies, including their eyes and even their tongues to express the song's meaning. Haka can express many messages, from mourning the dead to challenging an enemy. The New Zealand national rugby team, the All Blacks (named for their all black uniforms), perform a haka before their games. In this challenge haka, the players beat their thighs and chests and leap high into the air. Kiri Te Kanawa, a singer with Maori ancestors, performs a very different type of music. A soprano (singer with the highest range), she is one of the world's leading opera singers.

Despite their geographic isolation, New Zealand popular musicians have kept up with international music trends, and the country has a lively music scene. Dunedin is the country's music center. Some New Zealand bands, such as Split Enz, have become famous worldwide. Band members Tim and Neil Finn went on to solo careers when Split Enz broke up, and they also record together as the Finn Brothers. Besides being influenced by North American and European styles, some musicians have blended Maori music with Western styles for a uniquely New Zealand sound.

◉ Recreation and Sports

New Zealanders are sports enthusiasts—both as participants and spectators. One of New Zealand's most famous people, Sir Edmund Hillary, in 1953 was the first person to climb to the top of Nepal's Mount Everest, the world's tallest peak, along with Sherpa Tenzing Norgay.

Rugby, a fast and rough type of football played with no padding, ranks as the most popular sport. The national team, the All Blacks, plays international matches between June and September. Local rugby leagues are also popular.

During summer, most fans devote their attention to cricket—a

bat-and-ball game developed in Britain involving two eleven-member teams. Teams from overseas arrive in February and March to compete against New Zealand's best players. Soccer gained a large following when New Zealand athletes went to the World Cup competition in Spain in 1982, an accomplishment that remains a highlight in the country's soccer history. Hockey teams also meet competitors from other countries. Netball—a game similar to basketball—is a major women's sport. International netball tournaments take place in May and June.

New Zealand rowers and yachting crews have excelled in world competitions. In 2000 the America's Cup yachting events were held outside Auckland. The winning team is awarded the most famous trophy in the sport of yachting. Team New Zealand became the first yachting squad besides the United States to win the trophy twice in a row, in 1996 and 2000. In the 2004 Summer Olympics, New Zealanders earned two gold medals for rowing and one silver medal for canoeing. New Zealand also produces outstanding runners. Competing in Sweden in 1975, John Walker became the first person to

BUNGEE JUMPING

Modern bungee jumping was invented in New Zealand, inspired by the people of the Pacific island Vanuatu who jump off huge wooden towers with vines tied to their feet. New Zealander A. J. Hackett, with fellow speed skier Henry Van Asch, tested rubber cords and conducted a series of extreme jumps. In June 1987, Hackett gained international attention when he jumped from the Eiffel Tower in Paris, and the modern bungee jump was born. The world's first commercial bungee site, in 1988, was the Kawarau Bridge, 141 feet (43 m) above the Kawarau River, near Queenstown, New Zealand. Adventurous types can still jump there and at many other thrilling places in New Zealand.

run a mile in less than 3 minutes, 50 seconds. In the 2004 Summer Olympics, New Zealanders won one gold and one silver medal for the triathlon event (swimming, cycling, and running).

New Zealand's natural features lend themselves to outdoor sports, including white-water rafting and canoeing, camping, skiing, and tramping (the New Zealand word for hiking). Jogging was invented in New Zealand by runner and coach Arthur Lydiard, and remains popular. Sailing is also extremely popular, and many people own their own sailboat. The country's lakes, rivers, and coastal waters attract fishers from throughout the world. Horse racing is a popular spectator sport, and New Zealand breeders raise some of the world's finest horses. Many rural New Zealanders who own horses play a rugged version of polo.

◉ Food

With all the sheep in the country, it's no surprise that lamb (the meat of sheep less than one year old) is a favorite food. It is served in many ways, from barbecued lamb chops and sausages to roast leg of lamb with mint sauce. Mutton (the meat of adult sheep) is also eaten frequently, often in stews. Plain British cooking—hearty meals of meat and cooked vegetables—was a major influence on New Zealand cuisine, and many recipes are common to Australia too. Fish and chips (fish fried in batter with french fries) is a British fast-food tradition that was adopted by New Zealand. Meat pies are another favorite. In recent years, international cuisines, including other Pacific and Asian styles, have lightened the traditionally heavy food. A *hangi* is a traditional Maori earth oven in which food is cooked, as well as the name of a traditional Maori ceremonial feast. The coasts provide ample seafood, and the country's oysters, mussels, crayfish, and scallops are excellent. Toheroa soup is made from native clams.

RAINBOW KIWI SALAD

The juicy kiwifruit has emerald green flesh dotted with tiny black seeds. Its brown fuzzy skin is edible but is peeled for this recipe to make it prettier.

16 strawberries
½ cup blueberries
4 kiwifruits

1 large orange, or 1 can mandarin oranges, drained
½ cup yogurt (plain or flavored)

1. Wash the strawberries and blueberries gently in cold water. Drain, or lightly pat dry.
2. Peel and cut kiwifruits into round slices.
3. If using fresh orange, peel the orange, removing any pith (white rind). Slice the orange segments into bite-sized pieces.
4. Remove the strawberry stems, and slice the strawberries into thick wedges.
5. Layer the fruit into four individual glass serving dishes in the following order: orange bites, sliced strawberries, kiwifruit rounds, and blueberries sprinkled on top.
6. Stir the yogurt to make it creamy, and drizzle a little on top of each fruit dish.

Serves 4

Freshwater fish includes trout and eels. Smoked eel is a delicacy. Fresh produce includes kumaras that are served alone or with meat dishes. New Zealand is the leading producer of kiwifruits. Desserts include pavlova, a meringue (baked, sweetened, whipped egg whites) topped with kiwi or other fruit and whipped cream. As in Britain, cookies are called biscuits. Anzac biscuits, a kind of oatmeal cookie, are served on ANZAC Day, which commemorates those who served in World War I and other wars. Tea is the favorite drink. Cafes serving espresso and other coffee drinks are popular in big cities. New Zealand has a thriving beer and wine industry, and both alcoholic beverages are popular. There is even a kiwifruit wine.

 Visit www.vgsbooks.com for links to websites with additional information about New Zealand's culture. Learn about New Zealand's music, literature, movies, and traditional arts, as well as the influence Maori heritage has had on New Zealand's culture.

THE ECONOMY

Land is New Zealand's most important economic resource. Its productive agricultural sector requires many support services, including building and construction trades, transport, finance, processing, and trade sectors. The country depends on trade with other countries to sell its large agricultural output and to obtain the raw materials and manufactured goods it lacks. Historically, Great Britain bought most of New Zealand's meat, wool, and dairy products. Trade with Britain declined sharply in the early 1970s, however. New Zealand turned to other markets. In 1982 New Zealand and Australia signed the Closer Economic Relations (CER) Trade Agreement, eliminating all tariffs (import taxes) on goods sold by one country to the other. New Zealand's acceptance of the 1994 General Agreement on Tariffs and Trade (GATT) reduced some of the high tariffs other industrialized nations charged New Zealand to trade its agricultural products. In 1995 CER joined ASEAN (Association of Southeast Asian Nations) to encourage trade and

investment between the two areas. In the twenty-first century, Australia, the United States, and Japan rank as New Zealand's leading trading partners.

New Zealand has begun offering more types of goods and services to foreign buyers. Meat and dairy products still account for 30 percent of the nation's export earnings. But tourism, manufactured goods, fish, and timber products are increasing sources of income from abroad. New Zealand also has a small but growing film industry.

The average annual earning for New Zealanders, figured in U.S. dollars, is $20,550 per person. (In comparison, Australians earn an average of US $27,440.) New Zealanders pay personal income taxes, or a set percentage of their earnings, to pay for the costs of running their country. The government sets the tax percentage so that people who earn less don't have to pay as much. People with the lowest incomes pay 19.5 percent of their earnings as taxes. Those in the middle-income group pay 33 percent of their income, and the highest earners are taxed at 39 percent.

Agriculture

The agriculture sector of the economy, including farming, forestry, and fishing, brings in 8 percent of New Zealand's gross domestic product (GDP, the value of goods and services produced in a country during one year). About 55 percent of New Zealand's land area is used for agriculture. The higher hills provide pasture for hardy sheep, and farms on lower hills and flatlands raise cattle, sheep, and other livestock. Only about 6 percent of the farmland is cultivated for crops, and about 10 percent of the workforce is employed in this sector.

Most farmers own and live on their own farms. Their skilled, scientific approaches to agricultural breeding and management have led to highly productive, efficient farming. A mild climate allows animals to graze year-round in most areas of the country. The soil is not very fertile, however. European grasses were imported and, to be productive, grasslands require heavy applications of chemical fertilizer. Because much of the terrain is too steep for tractors, farmers spread fertilizer and grass seed on their pastures from airplanes and helicopters.

New Zealand is the world's largest supplier of lamb and mutton. After Australia, it is the second-largest exporter of wool, from the coat of sheep. About 90 percent of the country's raw wool is sold abroad. In addition to meat and wool, sheep provide sausage casing, skins, and tallow (fat). Although a few sheep stations cover many thousands of acres, most of New Zealand's farms are far smaller.

New Zealand has more than 3.5 million dairy cattle. Dairy farms, which average 100 acres (40 hectares), lie mostly in the Waikato and Taranaki areas of the North Island. New Zealand farmers pioneered the use of mechanical

MORE SHEEP THAN PEOPLE

New Zealand's 48 million sheep outnumber the nation's people by 12 to 1. The average flock contains about 1,800 animals, but some of the large stations in the high country of the South Island support 20,000 animals. The smaller sheep farms are family-run operations that employ outside help for seasonal tasks. Traveling groups of shearers usually clip the sheep. A good shearer can shave more than 300 animals per day. In the high country, shepherds patrol large flocks on motorized trail bikes and rely on dogs to help handle the flocks efficiently.

Many people consider **sheep** to be the most important animal ever domesticated, as they provide both meat and clothing. This sheep is being sheared; its wool will later be made into yarn for clothing.

milkers, and advanced equipment keeps these dairy farms among the most efficient in the world.

Factories convert most of the milk into butter, cheese, skim- and whole-milk powders, and other products. The New Zealand Dairy Board acquired and marketed dairy products abroad for many years. In 2001 Fonterra, which is one of the world's biggest dairy organizations, replaced the dairy board.

Besides dairy cattle, about 5 million cattle are raised primarily for meat. The beef sold for export is boned, cut, wrapped, and shipped in cartons to the United States and Canada.

Many farmers raise different types of animals to protect themselves when prices for cattle and sheep products are low. Goats furnish milk, meat, and a kind of wool called mohair. Red deer provide venison (deer meat) and hides for export.

New Zealand grows most of its own food. The country grows sufficient wheat, corn, peas, and potatoes to meet most of its needs. Barley is an important export crop. Leading fruit exports include apples, citrus fruits, nectarines, peaches, berries, avocados, and kiwifruit. Local vineyards grow grapes for making wine. Some of the

country's wines have gained international reputations.

⦿ Forestry and Fishing

The forestry industry has shifted from cutting down old-growth (original) forests to planting forests to harvest. Radiata pines—the main tree crop—thrive in plantations on the Volcanic Plateau, the center of timber production. Douglas fir and native evergreens, such as rimu, also provide a small amount of timber. Forestry industries represent 7 percent of the country's export income. The boom in wood products has stimulated businesses that serve the forestry sector, such as transport, vehicle repair, and construction. Pulp and paper companies turn out newsprint, paper, paperboard, wood panels, plywood, and particleboard. Forestry management programs ensure that timber supplies will continue to increase.

In the twenty-first century, fishing represents 4.5 percent of total export income. New Zealand exports 70 percent of its annual catch of seafood to Japan, Australia, and the United States. Trout and other freshwater species help the economy mainly by attracting sport fishers to New Zealand.

⦿ Industry, Mining, and Energy

Industry and manufacturing employ 25 percent of New Zealand's workforce and account for 23 percent of the nation's GDP. The country's factories provide an increasing range of industrial and consumer goods. The largest industries process agricultural products for export, including the processing of dairy products, paper, and other wood products.

Two companies produce steel, but New Zealand imports stainless steel to make equipment for the dairy, brewery, chemical, and forestry industries. A large facility at Bluff, on the South Island, makes aluminum for Asian markets.

A logging company collects cut logs on the South Island.

A number of plants in New Zealand assemble motor vehicles—mostly of Japanese origin. Other companies produce ships, tugs, barges, trawlers, and yachts. The plastics and textile industries manufacture a variety of consumer goods. Makers of leather goods and woolen carpets and textiles have abundant supplies of raw materials, and their products are major export items.

While most of New Zealand's minerals do not occur in large enough amounts to make mining profitable, the country does have an abundance of coal. Large supplies of phosphorite, for making fertilizer, also exist. Sands rich in iron ore are mined on the North Island's western coast. The iron is sold to domestic and foreign steel manufacturers.

Coal currently meets 11 percent of the nation's energy needs. Hydroelectricity stations, to harness the power of rushing water, provide 70 percent of New Zealand's electricity. A cable connects the main islands, so the more heavily settled and industrial North can use the extra hydroelectric power of the South. In some parts of the Volcanic Plateau, pockets of steam in the earth's crust are tapped to provide heat for homes and businesses.

The nation has large supplies of natural gas in the Kapuni Field in Taranaki and in the offshore Maui Field. New Zealand built the

This **hydroelectric dam** draws power from Lake Benmore, New Zealand's largest artificial lake. Hydroelectric power accounts for two-thirds of the country's power. Though cleaner than many other sources of power, hydroelectricity can negatively impact the environment. For instance, when Lake Benmore was created, it flooded more than 14,800 acres (6,000 hectares) of wetland and diverted much of the water from two nearby rivers, upsetting delicate balances in the ecosystem. To learn more about New Zealand's energy and natural resources, visit www.vgsbooks.com for links.

world's first plant where natural gas is converted into synthetic gasoline. The plant supplies about 50 percent of the nation's transportation fuel. Some of the gas is used to generate electricity, and some is converted into chemicals. New Zealand has several offshore oil wells, but it must import nearly all the petroleum it uses.

The Service Sector and Tourism

The service sector includes jobs that serve the general community, including jobs in government, education, health care, retail, trade, transportation, and tourism. This sector brings in 69 percent of New Zealand's GDP and employs 65 percent of its workers.

Tourism is a major and growing part of the service sector, employing about 10 percent of the workforce. Restaurants, hotels, and other services that support the tourist trade are significant contributors to the GDP. Almost 2 million people visit New Zealand every year. The greatest number come from Australia, followed by Japan, the United States, and Great Britain. New Zealand's natural beauty, its unusual geothermal features, and its unpolluted environment attract many tourists. Recreation-minded travelers take advantage of opportunities for skiing, tramping (hiking), rafting, fishing, and other outdoor activities. Through ecotourism, visitors can view wildlife in natural settings, but care is taken that the visitors do not harm the environment. Other visitors observe New Zealand's multicultural society and its advanced agricultural industries. In the twenty-first century, the world-wide success of three *Lord of the Rings* movies filmed in New Zealand has triggered a boom in tourists who want to see the scenery featured in the films.

New Zealanders travel frequently, taking regular vacations. Fourteen national parks and many forest, marine, and other types of parks and reserves cover about 12 percent of the country's land area and draw domestic, as well as foreign, vacationers. One of the largest national parks in the world is Fiordland National Park. This preserve, in the southwestern corner of the South Island, is known for its fjords, snowcapped mountains, forests, waterfalls, and lakes. Hundreds of tracks, or hiking trails, offer the best way to see New Zealand's natural beauty. Tramping and camping are well coordinated by the Department of Conservation.

RING BOOM

The Lord of the Rings trilogy was filmed and produced in New Zealand. Production costs, local employment, and increased tourism from the films' popularity brought about $400 million to the small nation. The New Zealand government actively markets its country as an attractive and less expensive alternative to making movies and television than the United States. Because the country has such varied geography, from green fields to bleak mountains, it can host stories that are set almost anywhere in the world. Fantasy pieces have been especially popular to make in the country, including the TV shows *Hercules: The Legendary Journeys* and *Xena: Warrior Princess*. Besides scenery, the availability of a skilled workforce and the relatively low cost of filming continue to attract film studios to New Zealand.

Transportation and Telecommunications

Despite its rugged terrain, New Zealand has an excellent highway system that includes more than 58,002 miles (93,341 km) of roads. Building this network required the construction of many bridges and tunnels—some 1 mile (1.6 km) long. There are about 2 million cars in New Zealand.

A railway system with 2,422 miles (3,898 km) of track links New Zealand's main cities. Freight and passenger services connect the two main islands with ferryboats that carry trains. Rail service is efficient but slow. Ferries also carry cars and passengers between islands.

The rugged terrain of the country encourages air travel. New Zealand has 113 airports, 46 of which have paved runways. Air New Zealand provides international and domestic air service. Many other air carriers also provide service to international airports in Auckland, Christchurch, and Wellington.

New Zealand's inland waterways are too swift and rough for boat transportation, but ocean shipping is efficient and competitive. The New Zealand Line sends cargo ships around the world. Vessels from other nations, however, carry most goods shipped from New Zealand's ports. The largest cargo ports are Auckland and Wellington on the North Island and Lyttelton (serving Christchurch) and Port Chalmers (at Dunedin) on the South Island.

New Zealand has an excellent communication system. Almost 2 million telephone lines and more than 2 million cellular phones keep New Zealanders in touch. Undersea cables link the country to Australia and Fiji, and two satellite earth stations are employed for international connections. More than 2 million people are Internet users, and thirty-six Internet service providers operate in the country. Hundreds of radio stations and dozens of television stations provide programming.

The Future

Although New Zealand's economic growth depends on the expansion of nonagricultural industries, farming will remain the foundation of the economy. As a small trading nation, New Zealand will continue to be affected by the rise and fall in world demand for agricultural products. The government of Helen Clark continues to aggressively pursue opportunities for trade in the global marketplace. Economic growth in the twenty-first century continues at about 3 percent, a slow but adequate rate.

The Maori and Pakeha populations have bridged some of their social and cultural gaps, but these two main groups continue to experience divisions. The unemployment rate is much higher for Maori than for Pakeha, and inequalities exist in wages and living standards. A continuing challenge for New Zealand is to improve educational and work opportunities for the Maori and to work out fair settlements for long-standing grievances over land.

New Zealand has also experienced some tension on the international front in its relations with the United States. The government risked damaging its friendship with the superpower in order to keep U.S. nuclear ships out of New Zealand's ports. The lack of support for the 2003 U.S.-led coalition against the Iraqi government of Saddam Hussein further strained military relations between the two countries. But while the two nations do not always agree on international issues, they basically have excellent and friendly relations.

New Zealand is a country of great scenic beauty. Its mountains, rivers, lakes, and coasts add to the quality of life of its people. Protecting their natural environment is important to New Zealanders. The reduction of government-provided social services challenges the country to protect high-quality health care and high educational standards for all its citizens as well. Achieving these goals while coping with economic and social demands will be a challenge in the twenty-first century. With its many natural resources, hardworking and well-educated population, the small nation looks well positioned to continue to meet that challenge with success.

Timeline

5,000,000 B.C. Earth movements form the islands of New Zealand.

ca. A.D. 700 The Maori people migrate from eastern Polynesia to the islands of New Zealand in canoes.

1100 Moa Hunter culture is established on the South Island of New Zealand. The Moa Hunters follow a simple way of life dependent on the large, flightless moa birds for food.

1300s The Moa Hunter culture begins to decline as the moa are overhunted.

1500s The Little Ice Age arrives. This is a period of cold and stormy weather that causes the further decline of the Moa Hunter culture.

1600s Maori on the North Island develop the Classic Maori culture, becoming skilled farmers, builders, weavers, and wood-carvers.

1642 Dutch explorer Abel Tasman reaches Golden Bay on New Zealand's South Island. Maori canoes attack the Dutch ship and the Dutch sail away.

1769 British captain James Cook arrives in New Zealand on the ship *Endeavour* as part of his travels exploring the South Pacific.

1790s Seal- and whale-hunting ships from Europe come to New Zealand's coastal waters. Australian and U.S. traders begin arriving, too, looking for timber and flax. Harbor villages begin to spring up.

1814 Samuel Marsden, a Church of England missionary, establishes the first Christian mission in the Bay of Islands area.

1820s Maori chief Hongi Hika attacks other North Island Maori with guns he received from the Europeans. Guns, diseases, and alcohol introduced by settlers greatly reduce the Maori population.

1823 Henry Williams translates the Bible into Maori and uses it to teach reading and writing to the Maori. Some Maori begin to convert to Christianity.

1840 Some Maori leaders sign the Treaty of Waitangi with the British government. The treaty makes New Zealand a colony in the British Empire.

1854 The national parliament meets for the first time. The Maori are the largest population in the colony, but only European, male landowners can vote for parliament.

1860 A dispute over land triggers the Land Wars—a series of armed confrontations between Maori resisters and the British.

1872 The British subdue the Maori fighters, and the Land Wars end.

1882 The new technology of refrigeration allows the first cargo of frozen meat to be sent to Great Britain, beginning a new era of trade.

1893   New Zealand women win the right to vote, the first women in the world to do so.

1906   Short-story writer Katherine Mansfield leaves New Zealand for Great Britain.

1907   New Zealand becomes a dominion—a self-governing country within the British Empire.

1918   By the end of World War I (1914-1918), about seventeen thousand New Zealanders have been killed in the fighting and many more wounded.

1935   The Labor Party comes to power during a worldwide economic depression. The new government establishes a welfare state.

1945   At the end of World War II (1939-1945), New Zealand becomes a founding member of the United Nations (UN).

1953   Edmund Hillary and climbing companion Sherpa Tenzing Norgay, from Nepal, were the first people to climb Mount Everest, the highest mountain in the world.

1973   New Zealand's major trading partner, Great Britain, limits its purchases outside of the European Community. New Zealand enters a period of economic crisis, including high unemployment.

1975   The Maori Land March treks from the far north to Wellington. The Treaty of Waitangi Act sets up the Waitangi Tribunal (court) to investigate Maori land claims.

1984   New Zealand bans nuclear ships, including U.S. ships, from New Zealand's waters.

1985   The Greenpeace ship *Rainbow Warrior* is bombed in Auckland, and one crew member is killed.

1987   A. J. Hackett introduces the modern world to the bungee jump when he bungee jumps off the Eiffel Tower in Paris. The Maori Language Act establishes Maori as New Zealand's official language, along with English.

1997   The National Party appoints the nation's first female prime minister, Jennifer Shipley.

1999   Labor leader Helen Clark becomes prime minister.

2000   New Zealand wins the prestigious America's Cup trophy for yachting for the second time. Alan MacDiarmid wins the Nobel Prize in Chemistry.

2004   The New Zealand film, *The Lord of the Rings: The Return of the King*, wins eleven Academy Awards, including Best Picture. Author Janet Frame dies. New Zealand wins five medals at the summer Olympic Games. A smoking ban and a civil union bill become law.

2005   New Zealand supplies aid to Southeast Asian areas hit by a devastating tsunami.

COUNTRY NAME New Zealand

AREA 103,736 square miles (268,676 sq. km)

MAIN LANDFORMS North Island, South Island, Stewart Island, Southern Alps, Volcanic Plateau

HIGHEST POINT Mount Cook, 12,349 feet (3,764 m)

LOWEST POINT sea level

MAJOR RIVERS Waikato, Wanganui, Rangitikei, Upper Wairau, Waitaki, Clutha

ANIMALS bats, frogs, skink, geckos, tuataras, albatrosses, bellbirds, kakapos, kea (mountain parrot), kiwis, penguins, pukekos (swamp hen), takahe (marsh hen), tui, weka (wood hen), deer, possums, rabbits, dolphins, marlin, sharks, sperm whales, tuna

CAPITAL CITY Wellington

OTHER MAJOR CITIES Auckland, Wellington, Christchurch, Hamilton, Dunedin

OFFICIAL LANGUAGES English, Maori

MONETARY UNITY New Zealand dollar (NZD). 100 cents = 1 dollar.

NEW ZEALAND CURRENCY

New Zealand dollar bills (paper money) come in 5-, 10-, 20-, 50-, and 100-dollar amounts. Coins are made in denominations of 5, 10, 20, and 50 cents, as well as 1- and 2-dollar coins. New Zealand has no 1-cent coins. Famous New Zealanders, including Kate Sheppard and Edmund Hillary, are pictured on the bills.

New Zealand adopted its flag in 1901. The British flag, called the Union Jack, occupies the top left corner, symbolizing New Zealand's historic link to Great Britain. On the right-hand side of the flag, against a blue field, are four red stars outlined in white. These stars form the Southern Cross, a constellation visible only in the night sky of the Southern Hemisphere.

New Zealand, unlike most countries in the world, has two official national anthems—"God Save the Queen," also Great Britain's anthem and rarely sung in New Zealand, and "God Defend New Zealand," which was given equal status in 1977. Thomas Bracken wrote the lyrics of "God Defend New Zealand" in the early 1870s, and John Joseph Woods composed the music. Recognizing the difficulty the average person might have singing the original music, the Ministry of Internal Affairs commissioned a new musical arrangement in 1979 for general use. A. Maxwell Fernie composed this optional music. The anthem is sung in both English and Maori. Below is the first verse of the song.

"God Defend New Zealand"

English Version	Maori Version
God of Nations at Thy feet,	E Ihow_ Atua,
In the bonds of love we meet,	O ng_ iwi m_tou r_
Hear our voices, we entreat,	_ta whakarongona;
God defend our free land.	Me aroha noa
Guard Pacific's triple star	Kia hua ko te pai;
From the shafts of strife and war,	Kia tau t_ atawhai;
Make her praises heard afar,	Manaakitia mai
God defend New Zealand.	Aotearoa

Discover what the melody of New Zealand's national anthem, "God Defend New Zealand" sounds like. Go to www.vgsbooks.com for links.

HELEN CLARK (b. 1950) Helen Clark, born in Hamilton, became New Zealand's first elected woman prime minister in 1999. (Jenny Shipley was the country's first woman prime minister, appointed in 1997.) A former political scientist, Clark was a leader of the Labor administration in the mid-1980s. She grew up in a farming family, and her personal interests include opera, reading fiction, tramping, and other outdoor activities.

EDMUND HILLARY (b. 1919) Sir Edmund Hillary was born in Auckland. He and climbing companion Sherpa Tenzing Norgay, from Nepal, were the first people to climb Mount Everest, the highest mountain in the world, in 1953. Hillary said he was an example of "the average New Zealander: I have modest abilities, I combine these with a good deal of determination, and I rather like to succeed." Hillary is honored on New Zealand's five-dollar bill.

RALPH HOTERE (b. 1931) Modern artist Hone Papita Raukura (Ralph) Hotere was born in Mitimiti, Northland. He trained in art education, and studied and painted around Europe in the early 1960s, developing his own unique style. Back in New Zealand, he began to have shows and to do collaborative works with New Zealand artists and poets. In 1979, for example, he used his friend Hone Tuwhare's well-known poem "Rain" to produce *Three Banners with Poem*. His work reflects political and social issues important to him, as well as personal experience and emotional states. His work speaks for itself, he believes, stating, "There are very few things I can say about my work that are better than saying nothing."

WITI IHIMAERA (b. 1944) Born in Gisborne, Ihimaera is a novelist and short-story writer who teaches creative writing at the University of Auckland. His novel *Tangi* was the first published novel by a Maori. A leading New Zealand author, he has also edited two books of the series Contemporary Maori Writing. His novel *The Whale Rider* was made into a film in 2003.

PETER JACKSON (b. 1961) New Zealand's most famous film director was born in Wellington. His first film was *Bad Taste*, made in 1987, and *Heavenly Creatures* was a modest international success in 1994. He featured the dramatic and beautiful landscapes of his country in the *Lord of the Rings* trilogy, which was a huge success. Jackson won Best Director at the 2004 Academy Awards for the final film of the trilogy, *The Lord of the Rings: The Return of the King*.

WIREMU KINGI (ca. 1795–1882) A powerful Maori chief of the Te Ata Awa tribe, Wiremu Kingi refused to give up tribal lands to the British. In 1860 he assembled an army of more than 1,000 Maori. At the battle of Puketakauere, his troops defeated about 3,500 British troops, one of the greatest victories of the Maori over the British. Eventually the British defeated the Maori, and Kingi moved inland.

ALAN MACDIARMID (b. 1927) Born in Masterton, MacDiarmid grew up and was educated in New Zealand. When he was ten years old, he borrowed a book called *The Boy Chemist* from the local library and kept it out for one year. As an adult, he taught chemistry at the University of Pennsylvania. In 2000 he was awarded the Nobel Prize in Chemistry for his discovery, working along with other scientists, that plastics could conduct electricity.

KATHERINE MANSFIELD (1888–1923) Born in Wellington, Mansfield moved to Europe when she was nineteen, where she wrote highly acclaimed short stories. Her stories are about everyday feelings and experiences, many based in her own childhood. She died of tuberculosis when she was thirty-four. She is New Zealand's most famous author, and her fiction is available in one book, *The Collected Writings of Katherine Mansfield*. Her journal has also been published.

COLIN EARL MEADS (b. 1936) Meads—nicknamed Pinetree—was a star player for the New Zealand national rugby team, called the All Blacks. His fame in New Zealand is equal to Babe Ruth's in the United States. He was born in Cambridge and grew up on a family farm.

FRANK SARGESON (1903–1982) Born Norris Frank Davey in Hamilton, this short-story writer, novelist, and playwright took the last name Sargeson partly in honor of his uncle Oakley Sargeson. In 1928 Frank had been arrested for homosexual encounters, then illegal, and went to live on his uncle's farm. He worked on the farm and wrote fiction, developing what he called "an appropriate language to deal with the material of New Zealand life." By 1940 he had more than forty stories published. In the 1950s, he wrote and directed plays, and in the 1970s wrote three volumes of autobiography. His final novel, *Sunset Village*, was published in 1976.

KATE SHEPPARD (1847–1934) Born in Liverpool, England, to Scottish parents, Kate Sheppard moved to New Zealand as a young woman and went on to lead the New Zealand woman's right to vote movement. She was a skilled organizer, speaker, and politician, and was known internationally as a worker for woman's rights throughout her life. Her picture is on the New Zealand ten dollar bank note.

TE ARIKINUI DAME TE ATAIRANGIKAAHU (b. 1931) Along with Queen Elizabeth of Great Britain, Queen Te Atairangikaahu, of the Waikato iwi, is the monarch of New Zealand. In 1966 she was chosen to be the first Maori queen by a gathering of chiefs, in succession to her father, King Koroki.

KIRI TE KANAWA (b. 1944) Born in Gisborne to a Maori father and a Pakeha mother, Kiri Te Kanawa went on to become a world-famous opera singer, known for her beautiful soprano voice. In 1981 she sang at the wedding of Prince Charles and Diana Spencer in Great Britain. She performs all over the world, and she has made many recordings.

THE CATLINS This is the name of the southern coast of the South Island. This region is full of ancient rain forests, waterfalls, and beaches, as well as home to a wide array of flora and fauna, including penguins.

FIORDLAND This area on the south west coast of the South Island includes Milford Sound, the most spectacular of the fjords. The Milford Track is one of the world's most famous hiking trails.

FOX AND FRANZ JOSEF GLACIERS On the west coast of the South Island, these glaciers come close to sea level. Visitors can walk on them or take a helicopter trip to view them from above.

KAIKOURA Located on the east coast of the South Island, this is the place to take whale-watching trips and go swimming with dolphins.

OTAGO CENTRAL RAIL TRAIL Running from Clyde to Ranfurly on the South Island, this old railroad track was turned into a car-free, easy walking or biking trail in 2000. The spectacular scenery changes frequently, and the trail passes through many tiny towns.

QUEENSTOWN This scenic city on the South Island is considered the capital of adventure sports, including skydiving and jet boating. Bungee jumping off the Kawarau Bridge is especially popular.

ROTORUA AND THE BAY OF PLENTY Called Sulfur City because of the smell of sulfur drifting up from the earth, New Zealand's thermal activity is on display around this North Island city at mud pools, geysers, and hot springs. The area around the nearby Bay of Plenty is also a center of historic Maori culture. Visitors can attend a Maori cultural evening, which includes a hangi, a Maori feast.

TONGARIRO NATIONAL PARK This World Heritage site located in the central plateau of the North Island offers some of the best mountain scenery in the country, with good hiking and skiing.

WAIPOUA KAURI FOREST On the west coast of the North Island, this forest is the home of some of the giant kauri trees, including Tane Mahuta, the Lord of the Forest. These are among the world's grandest and oldest trees. Some of them may be close to two thousand years old.

WAITOMO CAVES The area around Waitomo on the North Island is filled with limestone river caves, and the main Waitomo Cave has a glow-worm grotto where visitors can see thousands of these amazing insects that give off a luminescent blue light in the dark. Spelunking (cave exploring) trips are also offered.

Aotearoa: Maori name, the Land of the Long White Cloud, for New Zealand

colony: a country that is occupied and whose resources are controlled by people from another country. A British colony is part of the British Empire and ruled directly by Great Britain.

dominion: a country that is part of the British Empire but governs itself

ecotourism: a kind of tourism where visitors can view animals in their natural settings, but care is taken not to disturb the wildlife or surroundings. Money from ecotourism is used for conservation.

endemic: found only in a certain area or country

export: something of value sold and shipped to another country

fjords: narrow sea inlets that are bordered by steep coastal cliffs

geothermal: heat from underneath the earth

geysers: hot springs that send up jets of hot water and steam at regular intervals

gross domestic product (GDP): the value of the total output of a country's goods and services produced over a certain period of time, usually one year

haka: a Maori action dance with song

indigenous: original, or native, to a certain area

iwi: a Maori tribe

kiwi: a Maori word for the shy, flightless bird that is New Zealand's national bird. New Zealanders also use the nickname Kiwi to refer to themselves.

kumaras: sweet potatoes; traditional Maori food

Maori: native peoples of New Zealand. The people took the name, which means "normal," to distinguish themselves from the Pakeha.

Maoritanga: Maori traditional culture

marae: the open courtyard in front of a Maori meetinghouse (whare), where social and religious events are held

missionaries: religious teachers who work to spread their faith

moko: traditional Maori tattoo

Pacific Islanders: people from the central and southern Pacific islands, including Samoa and Niue; also called Polynesians

Pakeha: a Maori word referring to European settlers (non-Maori peoples)

rugby: a kind of football, played without padding

tapu: the Maori word that means "sacred." The English word *taboo* (forbidden because of social or religious reasons) comes from *tapu*.

tramping: Kiwi word for hiking

whare: Maori traditional meetinghouse

Adams, Douglas, and Mark Carwardine. *Last Chance to See.* **New York: Ballantine Books, 1990.**
Adams, author of the comic science-fiction best seller *The Hitchhiker's Guide to the Galaxy*, and zoologist Mark Carwardine took a series of journeys to see endangered animals, including the kakapo of New Zealand. Adams is smart, loving, and very funny in his depiction of the plight of these and other animals in peril.

BBC News. 2004.
http://news.bbc.co.uk **(October 20, 2004).**
The World Edition of the BBC (British Broadcasting System) news is updated throughout the day, every day. It is a good resource for up-to-date news coverage of New Zealand.

Central Intelligence Agency (CIA). "New Zealand." *The World Factbook.* **December 2003.**
http://www.cia.gov/cia/publications/factbook/geos/nz.html **(October 20, 2004).**
The CIA's *World Factbook* series provides statistics and basic information about geography, people, government, economy, communications, transportation, military, and transnational issues.

***Dictionary of New Zealand Biography.* N.d.**
http://www.dnzb.govt.nz **(October 20, 2004).**
This on-line dictionary of famous people (deceased people only) includes a section called Our Land, Our People. It presents snapshots of places, times, events, and trends in New Zealand history, which are linked to the biographical content.

***Economist.* 2004.**
http://economist.com **(November 6, 2004).**
The *Economist* is a weekly British magazine available online or in print editions. It provides excellent in-depth coverage of economic and political news from New Zealand and around the world.

***The Far East and Australasia, 2003.* London: Europa Publications, 2003.**
This annual guide provides coverage of New Zealand's physical and social geography, including articles and charts on the country's history, economy, and more. Australasia includes the regions of Australia, Tasmania, and New Zealand.

Harding, Paul, Carolyn Bain, and Neal Bedford. *New Zealand.* **Melbourne, Australia: Lonely Planet, 2002.**
Bursting with useful information, this travel guide offers in-depth coverage of the country's wildlife and wilderness, cities and activities, and is well illustrated with maps and color photos. It also offers a special section on Maori culture and arts.

***Kakapo Recovery Programme.* 2005.**
http://www.kakaporecovery.org.nz **(May 5, 2005).**
This site is all about kakapos (flightless parrots) and includes some of the eighty-six individually named birds in audio and video clips. The biographies of some of the people who work in the program to protect this highly endangered species are also provided.

Masson, Jeffrey Moussaieff. *Slipping into Paradise: Why I Live in New Zealand.* **New York: Ballantine Books, 2004.**

Masson is an author and scholar who chose to immigrate to New Zealand from the United States. In this overview of his adopted home, he covers the natural, political, and cultural history of the country, records a conversation with Edmund Hillary, gives an overview of Maori culture, and outlines his own personal travel recommendations. Maps, photos, glossaries, and recommended reading are included.

Population Reference Bureau. 2003.
http://www.prb.org (June 21, 2004).

The bureau offers reliable, current population figures, vital statistics, land area, and more. Special articles cover the environmental and health issues of each country as well as world population trends.

Shadbolt, Maurice. *Reader's Digest Guide to New Zealand.* **Sydney, Australia: Reader's Digest, 1988.**

Maurice Shadbolt is one of New Zealand's most celebrated authors. Shadbolt's informative and interesting text is accompanied by lavish photographs by Brian Brake. This is a guide to places, history, and culture of New Zealand.

Sinclair, Keith, ed. *The Oxford Illustrated History of New Zealand.* **Auckland, NZ: Oxford University Press, 1990.**

This book covers more than one thousand years of history with scholarly articles starting with the discovery of New Zealand by the Maori and including the social and cultural life of the nation. The illustrations are mostly historical photos.

U.S. Department of State. *Background Note: New Zealand.* **December 2003.**
http://www.state.gov/r/pa/ei/bgn/2791pf.htm (July 30, 2004).

This website provides facts about New Zealand's people, history, government, economy, and more.

Warne, Kennedy. "Hotspot: New Zealand." *National Geographic,* **October 2002, 75–101.**

A beautifully illustrated article that looks at the history of and the conservation efforts to save the endemic species of New Zealand.

Ball, Murray. *Footrot Flats.* **New Zealand: Hodder Moa Beckett, 1996.**
This favorite Kiwi comic strip about New Zealand farming life is told from the viewpoint of a sheepdog named The Dog. This edition is just one of many books of the Footrot Flats series.

Cousteau Society. *An Adventure in New Zealand.* **New York: Simon & Schuster, 1992.**
The Cousteau Society is an organization dedicated to the protection of the world's natural resources. Photographs from a Cousteau expedition to New Zealand introduce the reader to the ancient Maori traditions and the natural world of the country, from volcanoes to squid.

Ihimaera, Witi. *The Whale Rider.* **Orlando, FL: Harcourt, 2003. First published in 1987 by Reed Books.**
This novel by a Maori writer tells the story of Kahu, a girl in line to be the next chief of her Maori people, who have descended from a mythical "whale rider." But the current chief, her grandfather, doesn't believe a girl can be a leader. Kahu, however, proves him wrong when she shows she has inherited the ability to communicate with whales. This book was made into a movie in 2002.

Jackson, Peter, and Ian Brodie. *The Lord of the Rings: A Location Guidebook.* **San Francisco: Harper Collins, 2004.**
Since the success of The Lord of the Rings film trilogy, New Zealand has become "Middle-earth" to millions of moviegoers the world over. This guidebook showcases the main locations around New Zealand where all three films were shot. The book includes information about accommodation, food and entertainment suggestions, and interviews with key cast and crew.

Mahy, Margaret. *The Haunting.* **New York: Atheneum, 1983.**
Winner of the international Carnegie Medal, this novel by New Zealand author Margaret Mahy is the frightening story of Barney Palmer, who finds out that one person in each generation of his family is cursed. He has to discover if he has inherited supernatural powers.

Mallory, Kenneth. *A Home by the Sea: Protecting Coastal Wildlife.* **San Diego: New England Aquarium, 1998.**
Three New Zealand conservation programs are described and illustrated with full-color photographs in this book for young adults. The programs work to save Hectors dolphins, yellow-eyed penguins, and little blue penguins.

Maori Organisations of New Zealand
http://www.maori.org.nz
This site is a good place to start for links to all sorts of websites about the Maori.

Morrissey, Michael, Editor. T*he Flamingo Anthology of New Zealand Short Stories.* **London: Flamingo, 2000.**
This gathering of short stories is a collection of work by New Zealand's leading short story writers. It contains the work of twenty-one writers, frequently offering more than one story by each author. The anthology includes the work of Katherine Mansfield, Frank Sargeson, Janet Frame, Maurice Shadbolt, Witi Ihimaera, and more.

New Zealand
http://www.newzealand.org.nz
A beautiful and useful site that covers New Zealand's history, culture, tourism, photos, and sports.

New Zealand Government Online
http://www.govt.nz
This site offers general information about the country and the government.

100 % Pure New Zealand
http://www.newzealand.com
A site with information on New Zealand's history, culture, nature, as well as tourism information and a section on the *Lord of the Rings*.

Sammis, Fran. *Australia and the South Pacific*. New York: Benchmark Books, 2000.
The natural zones, regions, people, and cultures of New Zealand and other South Pacific nations are shown on maps and discussed in this title of the Mapping Our World series.

Smelt, Roselynn. *New Zealand*. New York: Marshall Cavendish, 1998.
Part of the Cultures of the World series, this illustrated book introduces the geography, history, religion, government, economy, and culture of New Zealand.

Stevenson, Andrew. *Kiwi Tracks: A New Zealand Journey*. Hawthorn, Australia: Lonely Planet Publications, 1999.
Andrew Stevenson spent four-months tramping (hiking) New Zealand's tracks (trails), including the famous Milford Track in Fiordland. He explores the country through its nature and through discussions with New Zealanders from all walks of life.

Te Kanawa, Kiri. *Land of the Long White Cloud: Maori Myths, Tales and Legends*. London: Pavilion, 1997.
Kiri Te Kanawa is a world-famous opera singer who grew up in New Zealand, the Land of the Long White Cloud. Her father was Maori and she grew up hearing stories and myths from Maori culture. She retells ancient tales that capture Maori culture and love of storytelling.

Theunissen, Steve. *The Maori of New Zealand*. Minneapolis: Lerner Publications Company, 2003.
Part of the First Peoples series, this colorful book offers nuggets of information about the Maori who settled New Zealand, from their arrival to their modern reclamation of traditional culture and heritage.

vgsbooks.com
http://www.vgsbooks.com
Visit vgsbooks.com, the home page of the Visual Geography Series®, which is updated regularly. You can get linked to all sorts of useful online information, including geographical, demographic, cultural, and economic websites.

Walsh Shepherd, Donna. *New Zealand*. New York: Children's Press, 2002.
Part of the Enchantment of the World series, this book is a good resource for facts, figures, and photos about New Zealand.

Index

arts and literature, 44, 47–52: film and media, 51; Maori art, 47–48; Maori tattooing, 48; music, 51–52; painters, 48–49; Queen Elizabeth II Arts Council, 44; writers, 49–51

agriculture. *See* economics and economy

Australia, 4, 7, 8, 24, 30, 31, 36, 40, 41, 54, 56, 57, 58, 60, 62, 64

bodies of water: Bay of Islands, 23–24, 27, 66; Cook Strait, 8, 10; Golden Bay, 23, 66; Hauraki Gulf, 18; Manukau Harbor, 18; Marlborough Sound, 10; Milford Sound, 72; South Pacific Ocean, 4, 6, 32, 41; Tasman Sea, 8, 12. *See* also fjords

cities (major): Auckland, 10, 13, 17, 18, 19, 25, 27, 28, 31, 32, 36, 39, 46, 49, 53, 64, 67, 68, 70; Christchurch, 13, 18–19, 25, 46, 49, 64, 68; Dunedin, 18, 19, 25, 52, 64, 68; Hamilton, 18, 19, 68, 71; Kororareka, 24, 25; Lyttelton, 19, 64; Queenstown, 54, 72; Wellington, 18, 19, 25, 28, 32, 35, 64, 67, 68, 70, 71

climate, 7, 12–13, 17, 20, 22, 26, 58

Clark, Helen, 33, 34, 64, 67, 70

Cook, James, 5, 23, 42, 66

cuisine (food), 21, 54–55. *See also* recipe

currency, 68

customs and traditions, 38–39, 51; of the Maori, 7, 20, 22, 24, 39–41, 44, 45–46, 48, 50, 51–52, 54, 55. *See also* arts and literature; cuisine (food); music

economics and economy, 7, 27, 28, 29–30, 31–33, 34, 36, 37, 39, 40, 42, 56–57: agriculture, 17, 21, 22, 28, 29, 45, 58–60; ASEAN (Association of Southeast Asian Nations), 56–57; Closer Economic Relations (CER) Trade Agreement, 56; economic boom and crisis, 28, 31–33, 60, 63; forestry and fishing, 60; industry, mining, and energy, 60–62; Rogernomics, 33; service sector and

tourism, 62–63; transportation and telecommunications, 63–64

education, 5, 7, 29, 31, 32, 34, 39, 43, 62, 64, 65; University of Auckland, 48, 70; University of Otago, 19

Elizabeth II (queen), 34, 71

fjords, 4, 9, 63, 72. *See also* geopolitical regions: Fiordland; bodies of water: Milford Sound

flora and fauna, 13–15, 16–17, 55, 59, 60, 72: bellbird, 15; cabbage tree, 14; cushion plant, 14; daisies, 14; forests, 13–14, 72; geckos, 15; giant moa, 14; kakapo, 15, 16, 17; karaka, 14; kauri tree, 14, 24, 72; kiwi bird, 15; kiwifruit, 55, 59, 60; pukeko (swamp hen), 15; nicotiana, 14; radiata pine, 60; red-blossomed pohutukawa, 14; silver tree fern, 14; skinks, 14; stoats (ermines), 16, 17; takahe (marsh hen), 15; totara, 14; tuatara, 15; tui, 15; weka (wood hen), 15

geographic regions: Canterbury Plains, 12, 18, 19, 26; Coromandel Peninsula, 10; North Island, 4, 8–9, 10, 12, 13, 14, 18, 21, 22, 24, 26, 27, 28, 36, 51, 58, 61, 64, 66, 68, 72; Northland Peninsula, 10, 23, 70; Southern Alps, 9, 12; South Island, 4, 8–9, 12, 13, 14, 18–19, 21, 23, 26, 28, 58, 60, 61, 63, 64, 66, 68, 72; Stewart Island, 8, 17, 68; Taranaki, 10, 27, 58, 61–62; Volcanic Plateau, 8, 12, 60, 61

geopolitical regions: Fiordland, 10, 72; Otago, 11, 12, 13, 19, 66, 72; Rotorua, 10, 40, 48, 72; Wairarapa, 8

geysers, 10, 12, 72

glaciers, 4, 12, 72; Fox glacier, 12, 72; Franz Josef glacier, 12, 72; Tasman glacier, 12

health care, 5, 7, 33, 39, 41–43, 62, 63; HIV/AIDS (human immunodeficiency virus/acquired immunodeficiency syndrome), 42–43; infant mortality rate, 42;

life expectancy, 40, 42
Hillary, Edmund, 52, 67, 68, 70
history and government: ANZUS
 Treaty, 31–32; British colonization,
 25–27; British Commonwealth, 30;
 Canberra Pact, 30; Great Britain's
 Privy Council, 35; House of
 Representatives, 27, 31, 32, 35;
 Land Wars, 27; the late twentieth
 century and the twenty-first
 century, 33–34; Maori people,
 20–22; modern governmental
 structure, 35; Pakeha people
 (Europeans), 23–24; social reforms,
 28–29; traditional Maori culture,
 22; Treaty of Waitangi, 5–6, 25,
 26–27, 32, 34–35, 47, 66, 67; World
 War I and World War II, 29–30
holidays, 47

islands. *See* geographic regions

Lange, David, 32–33

Maori, 39–41; art, 47–48; discovery
 and settlement of New Zealand,
 20; foods, 54–55; Maori Land
 Court, 35; Maori language, 41;
 Maori Language Act of 1987, 41,
 67; Maori Renaissance, 48–49;
 Maori Women's Welfare League,
 31; Moa Hunters, 21–22; music,
 51–52; religious culture, 45–46;
 traditional and modern literature,
 50–51; traditional Maori culture
 (Maoritanga), 7, 22, 39, 40, 41,
 44–45; Treaty of Waitangi, 5, 25,
 26, 30, 34–35, 47, 66, 67; Waitangi
 Tribunal, 32, 67
maps, 6, 11

marine life, 14
mountains, 9, 10, 11, 12; Mount
 Cook (highest point), 12; Southern
 Alps, 9, 12
music, 51–52

New Zealand: boundaries, location,
 and size, 8–9, 10, 11; court system,
 35; currency, 68; daily life, 37–38;
 ethnic diversity, 38–39; flag, 69;
 flora and fauna, 13–14, 68;
 government, 35; maps, 6, 11;
 national anthem, 69; neighbors, 8;
 population, 36–37; topography, 9:
 North Island, 10; South Island, 10.
 See also history and government

Pacific Islanders (Polynesians), 5, 18,
 30, 36–37, 38–39, 42, 44

recipe (rainbow kiwi salad), 55. *See
 also* cuisine (food); Maori: foods
religion, 44, 45–47; Christianity, 46;
 Hinduism, 46; Islam, 46; Judaism,
 46; Maori religious culture, 45–46;
 Ratana, 46
rivers and lakes (major), 12–13

sports and recreation, 52–53

Tasman, Abel, 5, 23, 66
Te Arikinui Dame Te Atairangikaahu
 (Princess Piki), 34, 71
treaties. *See* history and government;
 Maori

women and children, 7, 26, 28, 29,
 31, 34, 36, 39, 41, 42, 43, 47, 48,
 52, 67

Captions for photos appearing on cover and chapter openers:

Cover: The Champagne Pool at the Waiotapu thermal area outside of Rotorua

pp. 4–5 Hikers tramp the Sealy Tarns trail in Mount Cook National Park. Mount Cook, New Zealand's highest peak, is named after Captain James Cook, one of the first Europeans to have seen the mountain.

pp. 8–9 Milford Sound in Fiordland National Park is the most well-known fjord in New Zealand and is the only one accessible by road.

pp. 20–21 The Treaty of Waitangi was signed in this house on February 6, 1840. To read the treaty and learn more about the treaty's history, visit www.vgsbooks.com for links.

pp. 36–37 A group of schoolchildren take recess in the Maori village of Waima.

pp. 44–45 Maori men perform a traditional costumed war dance with weapons.

pp. 56–57 New Zealand's sheep outnumber the people living on the islands. Overall, there are about twenty-five times as many farm animals as people in the country, the highest animal to human ratio in the world.

Photo Acknowledgments

The images in this book are used with the permission of: © Warren Jacobs/Art Directors, pp. 4–5, 15 (main), 19, 23 (top), 40, 60, 62; © A. Tovy/Art Directors, pp. 8-–9; © Larry Dunmire/Superstock, p. 10; © Don Cole/Art Directors, p. 15 (inset); © STR/AFP/Getty Images, p. 17; © Eugene Schulz, pp. 20–21; © David Clegg/Art Directors, p. 23 (bottom); © Joan Wakelin/Art Directors, pp. 26, 56–57, 59; © Kamal Kishore/Reuters/CORBIS, p. 34; © Paul A. Souders/CORBIS, pp. 36–37, 43, 47; © Paul Souders|WorldFoto, p. 38; © Anders Ryman/CORBIS, pp. 44–45; © Robert Belbin/Art Directors, p. 46; © Ask Images/Art Directors, p. 48; © APOLLO MEDIA/ZUMA Press, p. 50; Daniel Berehulak/Pool/ Reuters/CORBIS, pp. 52–53; © Robin Smith/Art Directors, p. 61; Audrius Tomonis—www.banknotes.com, p. 68.

Front Cover: © Kevin Schafer; Back Cover: © NASA.